IMPORTANT NOTICE

The Forest Service has renumbered all of the forest roads in Western Washington.

The old numbering system was established over thirty years ago, before road planners had any notion of the maze of roads that eventually would be developed. The new numbering system should make road directions easier to follow.

Unfortunately, most maps still use the old numbers. For many hikes we have listed the old and new numbers side by side, so that old maps and new road signs can be used together.

100 Hikes in the
South Cascades and Olympics

Text: Ira Spring and Harvey Manning
Photos: Bob and Ira Spring

The Mountaineers
Seattle

THE MOUNTAINEERS: Organized 1906 "... to explore, study, preserve and enjoy the natural beauty of the Northwest."

0   9   8   7   6

5   4   3   2

Published by The Mountaineers, 306 Second Avenue West
Seattle, Washington 98119

Published simultaneously in Canada by Douglas & McIntyre, Ltd.
1615 Venables Street, Vancouver, British Columbia V5L 2H1

Manufactured in the United States of America

Edited by Barbara Chasan
Designed by Marge Mueller; maps by Helen Sherman, Gary Rands
    and Judith Siegel
Cover: Mt. Rainier and trail to Noble Knob, Hike #10
Frontispiece: Packwood Lake and Johnson Peak, Hike #42

Library of Congress Cataloging-in-Publication Data

Spring, Ira.
    100 hikes in the South Cascades and Olympics.

    Includes index.
    1. Hiking—Washington (State)—Guide-books.
2. Hiking—Cascade Range—Guide-books.   3. Hiking—
Washington (State)—Description and travel—
1981—   —Guide-books.   5. Cascade Range—Description
and travel—Guide-books.   6. Olympic Mountains (Wash.)—
Description and travel—Guide-books.   I. Manning,
Harvey.   II.   Mountaineers (Society)   III. Title.
IV. Title: One hundred hikes in the South Cascades
and Olympics.
GV199.42.W2S66   1985   917.97   85-15504
ISBN 0-89886-107-1

CONTENTS

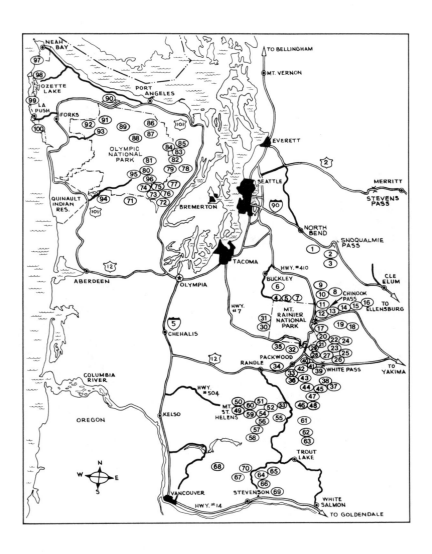

* These trails lie within the following proposed wilderness preserves:
    51–60 Dark Divide
    68 Siouxon
    69 Columbia Gorge
    71 Wonder Mountain
    72 Addition to Mt. Skokomish
The trails would become protected if bills to establish the wilderness areas are approved.

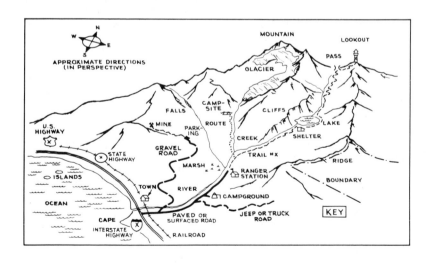

SAVING OUR TRAILS

Preservation Goals for the 1980s and Beyond

In the early 1960s The Mountaineers began publishing trail guides as another means of working "to preserve the natural beauty of Northwest America," through putting more feet on certain trails, in certain wildlands. We suffered no delusion that large numbers of boots improve trails or enhance wildness. However, we had learned to our rue that "you use it or lose it," that threatened areas could only be saved if they were more widely known and treasured. We were criticized in certain quarters for contributing to the deterioration of wilderness by publicizing it, and confessed the fault, but could only respond, "Which would you prefer? A hundred boots in a virgin forest? Or that many snarling wheels in a clearcut?"

As the numbers of wilderness lovers have grown so large as to endanger the qualities they love, the rules of "walking light" and "camping no trace" must be the more faithfully observed. Yet the ultimate menace to natural beauty is not hikers, no matter how destructive their great, vicious boots may be, nor even how polluting their millions of *Giardia* cysts, but doomsday, arriving on two or three or four or six or eight wheels, or on tractor treads, or on whirling wings—the total conquest of the land and water and sky by machinery.

Victories Past

Conceived in campfire conversations of the 1880s, Olympic National Park was established in 1938, the grandest accomplishment of our most conservation-minded president, Franklin D. Roosevelt. (Confined to a wheelchair and never himself able to know the trails with his own feet, FDR nevertheless saw the fallacy in the sneering definition of wilderness as "preserves for the aristocracy of the physically fit," knew the value of dreams that never could be personally attained.)

A renewal of the campaigns after World War II brought—regionally, in 1960—the Glacier Peak Wilderness and—nationally, in 1964—the Wilderness Act whereby existing and future wildernesses were placed beyond the fickleness of bureaucracies, guarded by Congress and the President against thoughtless tampering.

1968 was the year of the North Cascades Act, achieving another vision of the nineteenth century, the North Cascades National Park, plus the Lake Chelan and Ross Lake National Recreation Areas, Pasayten Wilderness, and additions to the Glacier Peak Wilderness.

In 1976 the legions of citizens laboring at the grass roots, aided by the matching dedication of certain of their Congressmen and Senators, obtained the Alpine Lakes Wilderness.

—And in 1984 the same alliance, working at the top and at the bottom and all through the middle, all across the state, won the Washington Wilderness Act encompassing more than 1,000,000 acres, including, in the purview of this volume, these new wildernesses—Clearwater, Norse Peak, William O. Douglas, Glacier View, Tatoosh, Indian Heaven, Trap-

Mount Rainier from Badger Peak

per, Wonder Mountain, Mount Skokomish, The Brothers, Buckhorn, and Colonel Bob—and additions to Goat Rocks and Mount Adams.

Is, therefore, the job done?

Goals Ahead

Absolutely not.

Had hikers been content with the victory of 1938 there never would have been those of 1960, 1968, 1976, and 1984. The American nation as a whole has a step or two yet to go before attaining that condition of flawless perfection where it fits seamlessly into the final mosaic of the Infinite Plan, and the same is true of the National Wilderness Preservation System. In the trail descriptions of this book we have expressed some of the more prominent discontents with the 1984 Act, such as omission of the proposed Dark Divide-Quartz Creek Wilderness; omission of Toutle, Muddy, and Upper Green River drainages from the Mount St. Helens National Monument; and lack of protection for the Pacific Crest Trail in the lower Greenwater valley and near Naches Pass and in several stretches between the Goat Rocks and Columbia River. Neither has protection been accorded certain other special places, such as the proposed Siouxon, High Rock, and Big Lava Bed Wildernesses, the Aiken Lava

Beds and superb forests adjoining the Mt. Adams Wilderness, and Conrad Meadows at the east edge of the Goat Rocks. Moving to the other mountain range treated in this volume, the Olympics, Lena Lake and the South Quinault Ridge were omitted from the 1984 Act, the also richly deserving Sitkum River was not included, and insufficient protection was provided for fisheries of the North Fork Skokomish, Hamma Hamma, and Dungeness Rivers.

However, it needs to be kept uppermost in mind that designation as "wilderness" or "national park" or "national monument" is a means, not the end. The goals ahead are not words on a document or lines on a map but the protection of the land these symbols may signify. Any other symbols that do the job are satisfactory. The *protection* is the thing.

In contrast to the immediate past, the preservationist agenda of the immediate future is focused less on redrawing maps than employing any practical method to preserve roadless areas from further invasion by machinery. In fact, we are now at a stage where the saving of trails, important though that is, has a lower priority than the saving of fisheries and wildlife resources, scientific values, gene pools, and another contribution of wildland too long neglected, the provision of dependable and pure water for domestic and agricultural needs.

What in the World Happened to Us?

The wheel is more than the symbol. It is the fact. The National Wilderness Act so recognizes by banning "mechanized travel," including *but not limited to* motorized travel; bicycles—"mountain bikes"—are excluded too, for the simple reason that in appropriate terrain they really can go 5–10 miles per hour, an "unnatural" speed often incompatible with the "natural" 1–3 miles per hour of the traveler on foot.

Outside the boundaries of dedicated wilderness, many trails can be amicably shared by bicycles and pedestrians, both capable of being quiet and minimally destructive and disruptive of the backcountry scene. Attach a motor to the wheels, however, and the route no longer deserves to be called a "trail," it becomes a *road*.

In the past quarter-century conservationists have been busy saving Washington trails by creating a new national park and a bouquet of new wildernesses. Meanwhile, the U.S. Forest Service, without benefit of environmental impact statements, has been assiduously converting *true trails* (that is, paths suitable for speeds of perhaps up to 5 or so miles per hour, the pace of a horse) to *motorcycle roads* (that is, "trails" built to let off-road vehicles—the ORV—do 15–30 miles per hour).

In this quarter-century the concerted efforts of tens of thousands of conservationists protected large expanses of wildland from invasion by machines—but during the same period a comparative handful of ORVers have taken away more miles of trails, converted them to de facto roads, than the conservationists have saved. As the score stands in 1985, only 45 percent of Washington trails are machine-free by being in national parks and wildernesses; of the other 55 percent, half are open to motorcycles—and thus are not truly trails at all.

When automobiles arrived in America the citizenry and government were quick to see they should not be permitted on sidewalks. The Forest

Service (and let it be added, the Washington State Department of Natural Resources, or DNR) are slower to recognize that whenever there are more than a few scattered travelers of either kind the difference in speed and purpose between motorized wheels and muscle-powered feet are irreconcilable.

Thinking to serve the laudable purpose of supplying "a wide spectrum of recreational opportunities," the Forest Service initially tolerated ORVs, then began encouraging them, widening and straightening and smoothing "multiple-use trails" to permit higher speeds, thus increasing the number of motors and discouraging hikers, in the end creating "single-purpose ORV trails"—in a word, roads.

Federal funds were employed for the conversion until that source dried up; since 1979 the Forest Service has relied heavily on money from the State of Washington Interagency for Outdoor Recreation (IAC), the subject of the following section of this book. Perhaps the most pernicious result is not the environmental damage, much of which can be repaired in time, but the appalling fact that when it accepts IAC funds the Forest Service signs a contract guaranteeing the trail or the equivalent to be kept open for ORVs in perpetuity. "Forever" surely is a major land-use decision, yet these conversations are made without environmental assessment, with only token public hearings, the notices tucked away in the fine print of small community newspapers.

Certainly, the Forest Service could not engage in such large-scale, long-term conversion of trails to roads if hikers were given the respect their numbers—overwhelming compared to the motorcyclists—deserve.

Hikers spoke up for the Washington Wilderness Act of 1984. By the many thousands they wrote letters to congressmen and senators. The pen is mightier than the wheel, and it must be taken up again, by those same tens of thousands, to write letters to congressmen and senators, with copies to the Regional Forester, Region 6, U.S.F.S., 319 S.W. Pine Street, P.O. Box 3623, Portland, Oregon 97208, asking that:

1. Trails be considered a valuable resource, treated as a separate category in all Forest Plans.
2. All trail users should be notified of public meetings concerning any Forest plan affecting trails; public meetings should be held in metropolitan areas as well as in small, remote communities near the trails.
3. To help reduce the conflict between hikers and ORVs, hikers on multiple-use trails (often with little children and heavy packs) shall have the right of way when meeting motors. For the safety of both parties, a speed limit of 7 mph shall be enforced on all multiple-use trails.

We do not concede that a "multiple-use trail" is a trail at all, but these measures can help ameliorate the present dangers, until philosophical retraining of land managers can be accomplished.

Harvey Manning

OF FEET AND WHEELS
AND POLITICS

The motorcyclists' "story" is that most trails are closed to machines. The reverse is true. Only 45 percent of the trail miles in the state of Washington are protected from motorcycles in national parks and national wilderness areas.

What of the other 55 percent, containing some of the best family hiking, some of the best early-season hiking, and some of the best bad-weather hiking? Already half of these are open to ORVs.[1] Whether they are open or closed to ORVs is the sole decision of the U.S. Forest Service, which in practice means the district ranger.

Motorcyclists say, "We have our rights. We want the same experiences hikers get. We want the same views."

Of course, they have "rights," both as to where they travel and their means of travel. However, the two must be separated. How much "right" does a motorcyclist have to disrupt the tranquility that other trail users have expended so much energy to find? Shouldn't motorcycles be allowed only where their speed and noise will not conflict with the rights of others?

As to "wanting the same experiences hikers get," unless they get off their wheels that's a foolish demand. There's no way to travel on a noisy machine at 10 to 25 miles per hour and get the same experience and appreciate the same view as quiet hikers traveling 2 or 3 miles per hour. Hikers have the physical challenge of traveling under their own power, have time to be scolded by noisy squirrels in the silent forest, to look at plants, and to fill their lungs with air untainted by the reek of hydrocarbons. As a fringe benefit—maybe the most important benefit—hikers strengthen their hearts, lungs, and legs. The sorry fact of the matter is that for many motorcyclists the only thrill of wilderness travel is the very act of dodging roots and rocks on a narrow trail at 25 miles per hour, surely a stimulating challenge, and not only to the motorcyclists but to the hiker on the same trail trying to avoid being run down or racketed to distraction or half-asphyxiated by exhaust.

In recent years, while the Forest Service has been asking for help from citizen volunteers in maintaining trails, and some trails have simply been abandoned for lack of funds, I have been puzzled by the number of trails already in good condition for hiking being "improved" for motorcycles, obviously with the expenditure of a lot of money. Researching Forest Service records, I found that a number of times as much as $50,000 or $100,000—once even $200,000—had been spent on individual trails to turn them into motorcycle paths.[2]

However, when I complained to the Forest Service that some of the money should be spent reopening popular car campgrounds that had been closed for lack of funds, building bridges for hikers, and upgrading some of the heavily used horse trails where the tread had been beaten to death, I was told they couldn't do that because the money was coming from unclaimed gas tax used by ORVs. The ORV Fund is administered by the State of Washington Interagency Committee for Outdoor Recreation (IAC). I couldn't understand that. After all, motorcycles use only one or two gallons of gas a day on the trails and would scarcely contribute more than 20 cents or, at most, 50 cents a day to the state in gas taxes. No matter how many there seem to be, there couldn't be enough motorcycles to pay for the cost of trail conversions I saw in progress.

Checking in Olympia, I found that in 1974 the State Department of Licensing conducted a strange survey of off-road travel and determined that 4.6 percent of all gas purchased in this state was for "off-road" recreational travel on roads not funded by the state gas tax. The survey showed that 1.3 percent of all the gas was used by off-road vehicles on non-roads. The State Legislature, confused as everyone else by the survey, set aside one percent of all state gas tax collected in an ORV fund with the stipulation that three-fourths of the money must be spent to the direct benefit of ORVs. If this survey is correct, in 1984 a relatively small number of ORV owners were using a mind-boggling twenty-four million gallons of fuel for their weekend recreation.[4]

My conclusion is that ORV people (four-wheel drives, three-wheelers, and various forms of motorcycles) contribute each year to the ORV fund $400,000 to $800,000 in unclaimed gas taxes[5] and another $164,000[6] in license fees. In return they get $3,000,000.[3] Certainly, hikers, hunters, fishermen, and families looking for a spot to picnic outnumber the actual ORVs by many times over. But they have been subsidizing the ORVers to degrade their own outdoor experience.

Early on, in the 1970s, the money was used to develop "ORV parks" on state, county or private land, but ORVs en masse are so disruptive that everyone ever subjected to having an ORV park in the neighborhood has complained bitterly, and making new ones has become virtually impossible. For example, in the late 1970s King County Parks put an ORV specialist (a dirt biker) on their payroll specifically to find a site in the county for an ORV park, and he drew up a list of some two dozen sites. However, the only site that did not arouse a storm of protests was a garbage dump (the sea gulls and crows were not questioned). King County therefore turned back to the state the funds it had been alloted.

There was so much money in the ORV fund that in 1978 the IAC turned to the Forest Service for help in spending it. From 1979 to 1984 the Forest Service was given $2,347,000[7] of state funds—our money—to ruin our (and the nation's—these are federal lands) trails for hikers. The Forest Service justifies these expenditures as improving multiple-use trails for everyone. However, encouraging motorcycles discourages hikers, so hikers stay away and multiple use becomes single-use motorcycle trails.

Why does the state subsidize ORVs? Because the ORV people were lobbying at the state capitol and the hikers were not.

In the state of Washington there are approximately 350,000 self-propelled hikers, and approximately 15,000 motorized trail users, so why, when hikers outnumber motorcyclists 20 to 1, is there a problem? In America it is the squeaky wheel that gets the attention. The motorcy-

Mesatchee Creek trail

clists, through their clubs and individuals, have squeaked loudly, while without a hiking organization to alert them, the majority of hikers has been quiet. It is no wonder the Forest Service assumes everyone is happy with motorcycles on trails and feels free to encourage more ORV use.

Hiking by its very nature is an individual activity done at one's own pace with one or two friends. Few hikers want to go out in large groups, so there is no incentive to join a hiking club. But without an organization to support them, hikers have had no voice. To fill this gap, two associations have been formed. New on the national scene is the American Hiking Society,[8] and on the local level is the Washington Trails Association.[9] These are associations, not clubs with meetings to attend. Their purpose is to watch over and to influence legislators and to keep their members informed of what is happening to trails.

In America the public has a chance to participate in decision making. The Forest Service has urged people, either in person or by letter, to become involved in its forest planning process. It is in this process that decisions are made on how many miles of trail will be eliminated by roads and how many trails will be opened to motorcycles. Unfortunately, in the past it has been the ORV organizations and motorcyclists who have responded, for without an organization to alert them, few hikers were aware of the meetings.

Only in America do involvement with federal agencies and letters to public officials accomplish so much. To influence policy at a national level, hikers must let their congressmen and senators know of their interest in trails. The Forest Service encourages hikers to be involved in its planning and reviews. If hikers want to save a favorite trail from logging or motorcycles, they must let the Forest Service know how they feel.

As an example of how warped an administrator's view of reality can be by supposed "fairness," many trails on the east slopes of the Cascades that are closed to wheels in their upper reaches, are open to them for some distance from the trailhead. What this means is that senior citizens, and families with small children, who can only manage a few miles a day, must do their walking on motorcycle roads.

Besides keeping informed by joining hiking organizations, hikers must speak for themselves, must take up their pens—their pencils—their typewriters—their word-processors—their telephones. With whatever tool, hikers must speak! Voice (or better yet write) your opinions to your congressmen on how trails should be used. Contact your state senators and representatives and let them know how you feel about the state subsidizing ORVs. Don't just stand aside, *do something*. Then send a note or copy of your letters to the regional forester.[10]

Ira Spring

---

1 *Washington State Interagency for Outdoor Recreation's report, "ORV Dollars and You," 1985.*

2 *Wenatchee National Forest's request for ORV funds, September 1984.*

3 *Washington State Department of Licensing report, "1984 Washington State Motor Fuel Distribution."*

4 *Others have noticed this inequity. Washington State Governor's "Recreation Resource Advisory Committee's 1984 Final Report," page 15.*

5 *Estimate only. No accurate survey has ever been made.*

6 *Washington State Department of Licensing.*

7 *IAC Off-Road Vehicle Program 1978–1984, letter dated December 1984.*

8 *American Hiking Society, 1701 18th Street N.W., Washington, D.C. 20009.*

9 *Washington Trails Association, 16812 36th West, Lynnwood, WA 98037.*

10 *Regional Forester, Region 6, USFS, 319 S.W. Pine Street, P.O. Box 3623, Portland, OR 97208.*

INTRODUCTION

The country sampled by these 100 hikes has many characteristics in common throughout, and in common, too, with companion volumes on the region north of Snoqualmie Pass, *100 Hikes in the Alpine Lakes* and *100 Hikes in the North Cascades,* as well as the volume devoted entirely to The Mountain, *50 Hikes in Mount Rainier National Park.* There are, however, significant differences from place to place caused by variations in climate, geology, elevation, and the amount and sort of human use.

Each of this book's two major provinces breaks more or less distinctly into subprovinces. The Olympic Mountains have an "ocean side"—the wet west and south slopes where storms from the Pacific wash ashore like so many giant waves on a beach—and a "rainshadow side"—the relatively arid north and west where the clouds are mainly empties. The two merge in the middle of the range, where the distances of 55–85 west-east miles from ocean to Hood Canal and roughly 70 south-north miles from foothills to Strait of Juan de Fuca give room for a spacious wilderness of glaciers and crags and flower fields, rainforests and subalpine parklands and alpine tundras, and one of the largest wildlife populations in America.

The term "South Cascades" requires explanation, since by one usage all the Cascades in Washington are "North" and the "South" lie beyond the "Oregon" Cascades, in California. In the terminology nowadays most accepted in Washington, "North" is from Stevens Pass to Canada, "Alpine Lakes" is between Stevens Pass and Snoqualmie Pass, and from there to the Columbia River is "South."

The first of the subprovinces, south from Snoqualmie Pass, is the least alpine stretch of the state's Cascade Crest and is more densely inhabited by logging trucks and talkie-tooters than hikers, who find few attractions except the Pacific Crest National Scenic Trail, leading from one scenic clearcut to another.

As Rainier, set off west of the crest, rises higher and sprawls wider in the eye of the south-walking traveler, the main line of the range thrusts up the craggy peaks and bright meadows of the Norse Peak Wilderness. Where this unit ends, at Chinook Pass, the William O. Douglas Wilderness begins, extending south to White Pass, west into storm-wet, rain-green, ice-white Mount Rainier National Park, and east to rattlesnake prairies of Central Washington where desert and alpine plants blossom side by side.

From White Pass south the story is all volcanoes: The ancient, deep-dissected ruins of a fire mountain once perhaps on the scale of Adams, in the Goat Rocks Wilderness; Adams, outbulked only by Rainier, in the Mount Adams Wilderness; a landscape spattered with cinder cones and smoothed by lava flows, some eroded and forested, as in the Trapper Wilderness, others high and meadowed, as in the Indian Heaven Wilderness; and never to be ignored, not even before 1980, the centerpiece of the Mount St. Helens National Volcanic Monument.

Within the subprovinces of the Olympics and South Cascades are an infinity of trail experiences—short and easy hikes that can be done by small children and elders with no training or equipment for mountain travel, and long hikes, and difficult hikes, and long-and-difficult off-trail hikes which should be attempted only by the hardiest of wilderness roamers.

The hiking season in low-elevation valleys of the Olympics—and on the zero-elevation beaches—is the whole year; higher, the flowers may not poke through snowbanks until late July, a mere several weeks before their frozen seeds are blanketed by the new winter's white; higher still there are no flowers ever, and no real hiking season, either, only a climbing season. There are places on the east slope of the Cascades where on any day of the year a person has an 85 percent chance of a sunburn, and others, on the west slope of the Olympics, where on any day of the year a person has an 85 percent chance of getting soaking wet right through his rubber boots and rainproof parka, and others, as on the Cascade Crest, where hikers within a mile of each other are at one and the same time gasping from thirst (east) and sputtering like a whale (west).

Administration

The two provinces are administered by the National Park Service and by the U.S. Forest Service in the Wenatchee, Gifford Pinchot, and Olympic National Forests. Because regulations on use vary, hikers should be aware of which administrative units they are traveling.

Mount Rainier and Olympic National Parks have been set aside, to use the words of the National Park Act of 1916, "to conserve the scenery and the natural and historic objects and wildlife . . . " Each visitor must therefore enjoy the Parks "in such manner and by such means as will leave them unimpaired for the enjoyment of future generations." A good motto for Park users is: "Take only a picture, leave only a footprint."

Much of both Parks soon will be dedicated as wilderness, so that not only the National Park Act of 1916 but the Wilderness Act of 1964 will apply, giving a still higher degree of protection. Motorized (and mechanized, including "mountain bikes") travel on Park trails is forbidden and horse travel closely regulated. Hunting is banned—but not fishing. Pets are not allowed on trails, since their presence disturbs wildlife.

Backcountry permits are required for all overnight hikers in National Parks, and may be obtained at ranger stations on the entry roads.

Under U.S. Forest Service jurisdiction are the Goat Rocks, Mt. Adams, Clearwater, Glacier View, Tatoosh, Trapper, Indian Heaven, William O. Douglas, and Norse Peak Wildernesses, where "the earth and its community of life are untrammeled by man, where man himself is a visitor who does not remain." Motorized (and mechanized) travel is forbidden absolutely and horse travel is beginning to be regulated or even eliminated at some points; foot travel and camping are currently less restricted, though the backcountry population explosion will require increasing controls to protect the fragile ecosystems.

Also under the Forest Service is the Mount St. Helens National Volcanic Monument, where management plans are still evolving, one wary ear always cocked to hear what more the volcano may have to say on the subject.

Maps

Each hike description in this book lists the appropriate topographic maps (if such are available) published by the U.S. Geological Survey. These can be purchased at mountain equipment shops or map stores or by writing the U.S. Geological Survey, Federal Center, Denver, Colorado 80225. The USGS maps are the hiker's best friend.

The National Forests publish recreation maps which are quite accurate and up-to-date. Excellent topographic maps are available for the Goat Rocks and Mt. Adams Wildernesses. These maps may be obtained for a small fee at ranger stations or by writing the Forest Supervisors at:

Mt. Baker-Snoqualmie National Forest
1022 1st Avenue
Seattle, WA 98104

Wenatchee National Forest
P.O. Box 811
Wenatchee, WA 98801

Gifford Pinchot National Forest
500 W. 12th Street
Vancouver, WA 98660

Olympic National Forest
Federal Building
Olympia, WA 98501

In the National Forests a traveler not only must have a map published by the Forest Service but it must be a *current* map; many an aging hiker seeking to revisit trails of his youth and equipped solely with old maps and memories has gotten lost in the much-clearcut valleys of Gifford Pinchot National Forest and wandered bewildered until he ran out of gas. (Watch along roadsides for bleached bones of Kelties and Volkswagen beetles.)

The problem—and it is a distinct pain in the lower back—is that the Forest Service is engaged in renumbering roads, made necessary when the number of roads grew so large as to require the use of more than three digits. For instance, road No. 130 became road No. 1200830, and is perhaps shown as such on the new map, though the roadside sign may be simply "830." One ranger district is using parentheses, as 1200(830), another dashes, as 1200–830, and another commas, as 1200,830.

A traveler *must* know the right numbers because in many areas the Forest Service puts no names on signs, just numbers—the new ones. Your map, if it has the old numbers, will merely deepen your confusion.—And we hate to mention it, but many of the old signs remain, with the old numbers, so that even your *new* map compounds the difficulty. A word to the wise: particularly in the South Cascades, never leave civilization without a full tank of gas, survival rations, and instructions to family or friends on when to call out the Logging Road Search and Rescue Team.

Clothing and Equipment

Many trails described in this book can be walked easily and safely, at least along the lower portions, by any person capable of getting out of a car and onto his feet, and without any special equipment whatever.

To such people we can only say, "welcome to walking—but beware!" Northwest mountain weather, especially on the ocean side of the ranges, is notoriously undependable. Cloudless morning skies can be followed by afternoon deluges of rain or fierce squalls of snow. Even without a storm a person can get mighty chilly on high ridges when—as often happens—a cold wind blows under a bright sun and pure blue sky.

No one should set out on a Cascade or Olympic trail, unless for a brief stroll, lacking warm long pants, wool (or the equivalent) shirt or sweater, and a windproof and rain-repellent parka, coat, or poncho. (All these in the rucksack, if not on the body during the hot hours.) And on the feet— sturdy shoes or boots plus two pair of wool socks and an extra pair in the rucksack.

As for that rucksack, it should also contain the Ten Essentials, found to be so by generations of members of The Mountaineers, often from sad experience:

1. Extra clothing—more than needed in good weather.
2. Extra food—enough so something is left over at the end of the trip.
3. Sunglasses—necessary for most alpine travel and indispensable on snow.
4. Knife—for first aid and emergency firebuilding (making kindling).
5. Firestarter—a candle or chemical fuel for starting a fire with wet wood.
6. First aid kit.
7. Matches—in a waterproof container.
8. Flashlight—with extra bulb and batteries.
9. Map—be sure it's the right one for the trip.
10. Compass—be sure to know the declination, east or west.

Camping and Fires

Indiscriminate camping blights alpine meadows. A single small party may trample grass, flowers, and heather so badly they don't recover from the shock for several years. If the same spot is used several or more times a summer, year after year, the greenery vanishes, replaced by bare dirt. The respectful traveler always aims to camp in the woods, or in rocky morainal areas. These alternatives lacking, it is better to use a meadow site already bare—in technical terminology, "hardened"—rather than extend the destruction into virginal places nearby.

Particularly to be avoided are camps on soft meadows (hard rock or bare-dirt sites may be quite all right) on the banks of streams and lakes. Delightful and scenic as such sites are, their use may endanger the water purity, as well as the health of delicate plants. Moreover, a camp on a viewpoint makes the beauty unavailable to other hikers who simply want to come and look, or eat lunch, and then go camp in the woods.

Carry a collapsible water container to minimize the trips to the water supply that beat down a path. (As a bonus, the container lets you camp high on a dry ridge, where the solitude and the views are.)

Carry a lightweight pair of camp shoes, less destructive to plants and soils than trail boots.

As the age of laissez faire camping yields to the era of thoughtful management, different policies are being adopted in different places. For example, high-use spots may be designated "Day Use Only," forbidding camps. In others there is a blanket rule against camps within 100 feet of the water. However, in certain areas the rangers have inventoried existing camps, found 95 percent are within 100 feet of the water, and decided it is better to keep existing sites, where the vegetation long since has been gone, than to establish new "barrens" elsewhere. The rule in such places is "use established sites"; wilderness rangers on their rounds disestablish those sites judged unacceptable.

Few shelter cabins remain—most shown on maps aren't there anymore—so always carry a tent or tarp. *Never* ditch the sleeping area unless and until essential to avoid being flooded out—and afterward be sure to fill the ditches, carefully replacing any sod that may have been dug up.

Always carry a sleeping pad of some sort to keep your bag dry and your bones comfortable. *Do not* revert to the ancient bough bed of the frontier past.

The wood fire also is nearly obsolete in the high country. At best, dry firewood is hard to find at popular camps. What's left, the picturesque silver snags and logs, is part of the scenery, too valuable to be wasted cooking a pot of soup. It should be (but isn't quite, what with the survival of little hatchets and little folks who love to wield them) needless to say that green, living wood must never be cut; it doesn't burn anyway.

Both for reasons of convenience and conservation, the highland hiker should carry a lightweight stove for cooking (or not cook—though the food is cold, the inner man is hot) and depend on clothing and shelter (and sunset strolls) for evening warmth. The pleasures of a roaring blaze on a cold mountain night are indisputable, but a single party on a single night may use up ingredients of the scenery that were long decades in growing, dying, and silvering.

At remote backcountry camps, and in forests, fires perhaps may still be built with a clear conscience. Again, one should minimize impact by using only established fire pits and using only dead and down wood. When finished, be certain the fire is absolutely out—drown the coals and stir them with a stick and then drown the ashes until the smoking and steaming have stopped completely and a finger stuck in the slurry feels no heat. Embers can smoulder underground in dry duff for days, spreading gradually and burning out a wide pit—or kindling trees and starting a forest fire.

If you decide to build a fire, *do not make a new fire ring*—use an existing one. In popular areas patroled by rangers, its existence means this is an approved, "established" or "designated" campsite. If a fire ring has been heaped over with rocks, it means the site has been dis-established.

Litter and Garbage and Sanitation

Ours is a wasteful, throwaway civilization—and something is going to have to be done about that soon. Meanwhile, it is bad wildland manners to leave litter for others to worry about. The rule among considerate hikers is: *If you can carry it in full, you can carry it out empty.*

Thanks to a steady improvement in manners over recent decades, and the posting of wilderness rangers who glory in the name of garbage-collectors, American trails are cleaner than they have been since Columbus landed. Every hiker should learn to be a happy collector.

On a day hike, take back to the road (and garbage can) every last orange peel and gum wrapper.

On an overnight or longer hike, burn all paper (if a fire is built) but carry back all unburnables, including cans, metal foil, plastic, glass, and papers that won't burn.

Don't bury garbage. If fresh, animals will dig it up and scatter the remnants. Burning before burying is no answer either. Tin cans take as long as 40 years to disintegrate completely; aluminum and glass last for centuries. Further, digging pits to bury junk disturbs the ground cover, and iron eventually leaches from buried cans and "rusts" springs and creeks.

Don't leave leftover food for the next travelers; they will have their own supplies and won't be tempted by "gifts" spoiled by time or chewed by animals.

Especially don't cache plastic tarps. Weathering quickly ruins the fabric, little creatures nibble, and the result is a useless, miserable mess.

Keep the water pure. Don't wash dishes in streams or lakes, loosing food particles and detergent. Haul buckets of water off to the woods or rocks, and wash and rinse there. Eliminate body wastes in places well removed from watercourses; first dig a shallow hole in the "biological disposer layer," then touch a match to the toilet paper (or better, use leaves), and finally cover the evidence. So managed, the wastes are consumed in a matter of days. Where privies are provided, use them.

Party Size

One management technique used to minimize impact in popular areas is to limit the number of people in any one group to a dozen or fewer. Hikers with very large families (or outing groups from clubs or wherever) should check the rules when planning a trip.

Pets

The handwriting is on the wall for dog owners. Pets always have been forbidden on national park trails and now some parts of wildernesses are being closed. How fast the ban spreads will depend on the owners' sensitivity, training, acceptance of responsibility, and courtesy—and on the expressed wishes of non-owners.

Where pets are permitted, even a well-behaved dog can ruin someone else's trip. Some dogs noisily defend an ill-defined territory for their master, "guard" him on the trail, snitch enemy bacon, and are quite likely to defecate on the flat bit of ground the next hiker will want to sleep on.

For a long time to come there will be plenty of "empty" country for those who hunt upland game with dogs or who simply can't enjoy a family outing without ol' Rover. However, the family that wants to go where the crowds are must leave its best friend home.

Do not depend on friendly tolerance of wilderness neighbors. Some people are so harassed at home by loose dogs that a hound in the wilderness has the same effect on them as a motorcycle. They may holler at you and turn you in to the ranger.

Dogs belong to the same family as coyotes, and even if no wildlife is visible, a dog's presence is sensed by the small wild things into whose home it is intruding.

Horses

As backcountry population grows the trend is toward designating certain trails and camps "Hiker Only," because some ecosystems cannot withstand the impact of large animals and some trails are not safe for them. However, many wilderness trails will continue to be "Hiker and Horse" (no motorcycles, no "mountain bikes") and the two must learn to get along.

Most horse riders do their best to be good neighbors on the trail and know how to go about it. The typical hiker, though, is ignorant of the difficulties inherent in maneuvering a huge mass of flesh (containing a very small brain) along narrow paths on steep mountains.

The first rule is, the horse has the right of way. For his own safety as well as that of the rider, the hiker must get off the trail—on the downhill side, preferably, giving the clumsy animal and its perilously-perched rider the inside of the tread. If necessary—as, say, on the Goat Rocks Crest—retreat some distance to a safe passing point.

The second rule is, when you see the horse approaching, do not keep silent or stand still in a mistaken attempt to avoid frightening the beast. Continue normal motions and speak to it, so the creature will recognize you as just another human and not think you a silent and doubtless dangerous monster.

Finally, if you have a dog along, get a tight grip on its throat to stop the nipping and yapping, which may endanger the rider and, in the case of a surly horse, the dog as well.

Theft

A quarter-century ago theft from a car left at the trailhead was rare. Not now. Equipment has become so fancy and expensive, so much worth stealing, and hikers so numerous, their throngs creating large assemblages of valuables, that theft is a growing problem. Not even wilderness camps are entirely safe; a single raider hitting an unguarded camp may easily carry off several sleeping bags, a couple tents and assorted stoves, down booties, and freeze-dried strawberries—maybe $1000 worth of gear in one load! However, the professionals who do most of the stealing mainly concentrate on cars. Authorities are concerned but can't post guards at every trailhead.

Rangers have the following recommendations.

First and foremost, don't make crime profitable for the pros. If they break into a hundred cars and get nothing but moldy boots and tattered T shirts they'll give up. The best bet is to arrive in a beat-up 1960 car with doors and windows that don't close and leave in it nothing of value. If you insist on driving a nice new car, at least don't have mag wheels, tape deck, and radio, and keep it empty of gear. Don't think locks help—pros can open your car door and trunk as fast with a picklock as you can with your key. Don't imagine you can hide anything from them—they know all the hiding spots. If the hike is part of an extended car trip, arrange to store your extra equipment at a nearby motel.

Be suspicious of anyone waiting at a trailhead. One of the tricks of the trade is to sit there with a pack as if waiting for a ride, watching new arrivals unpack—and hide their valuables—and maybe even striking up a conversation to determine how long the marks will be away.

The ultimate solution, of course, is for hikers to become as poor as they were in the olden days. No criminal would consider trailheads profitable if the loot consisted solely of shabby khaki war surplus.

Safety Considerations

The reason the Ten Essentials are advised is that hiking in the back-country entails unavoidable risk that every hiker assumes and must be aware of and respect. The fact that a trail is described in this book is not a representation that it will be safe for you. Trails vary greatly in difficulty and in the degree of conditioning and agility one needs to enjoy them safely. On some hikes routes may have changed or conditions may have deteriorated since the descriptions were written. Also, trail conditions can change even from day to day, owing to weather and other factors. A trail that is safe on a dry day or for a highly conditioned, agile, properly equipped hiker may be completely unsafe for someone else or unsafe under adverse weather conditions.

You can minimize your risks on the trail by being knowledgeable, prepared and alert. There is not space in this book for a general treatise on safety in the mountains, but there are a number of good books and public courses on the subject and you should take advantage of them to increase your knowledge. Just as important, you should always be aware of your own limitations and of conditions existing when and where you are hiking. If conditions are dangerous, or if you are not prepared to deal with them safely, choose a different hike! It's better to have a wasted drive than to be the subject of a mountain rescue.

These warnings are not intended to scare you off the trails. Hundreds of thousands of people have safe and enjoyable hikes every year. However, one element of the beauty, freedom and excitement of the wilderness is the presence of risks that do not confront us at home. When you hike you assume those risks. They can be met safely, but only if you exercise your own independent judgement and common sense.

Protect This Land, Your Land

The Cascade and Olympic country is large and rugged and wild—but it is also, and particularly in the scenic climaxes favored by hikers, a fragile country. If man is to blend into the ecosystem, rather than dominate and destroy, he must walk lightly, respectfully, always striving to make his passage through the wilderness invisible.

The public servants entrusted with administration of the region have a complex and difficult job and they desperately need the cooperation of every wildland traveler. Here, the authors would like to express appreciation to these dedicated men for their advice on what trips to include in this book and for their detailed review of the text and maps. Thanks are due the Superintendent of Olympic National Park, the Supervisors of the Wenatchee, Gifford Pinchot, and Olympic National Forests, and their district rangers and other staff members.

On behalf of the U.S. Forest Service and National Park Service and The Mountaineers, we invite Americans—and all citizens of Earth—to come and see and live in their Washington Cascades and Olympics, and while enjoying some of the world's finest wildlands, to vow henceforth to share in the task of preserving the trails and ridges, lakes and rivers, forests and flower gardens for future generations, our children and grandchildren, who will need the wilderness experience at least as much as we do, and probably more.

Water

Hikers traditionally have drunk the water in wilderness in confidence, doing their utmost to avoid contaminating it so the next person also can safely drink. But there is no assurance your predecessor has been so careful.

No open water ever, nowadays, can be considered certainly safe for human consumption. Any reference in this book to "drinking water" is not a guarantee. It is entirely up to the individual to judge the situation and decide whether to take a chance.

In the late 1970s began a great epidemic of giardiasis, caused by a vicious little parasite that spends part of its life cycle swimming free in water, part in the intestinal tract of beavers and other wildlife, dogs, and people. Actually, the "epidemic" was solely in the press; *Giardia* were first identified in the 18th century and are present in the public water system of many cities of the world and many towns in America—including some in the foothills of the Cascades. Long before the "outbreak" of "beaver fever" there was the well-known malady, the "Boy Scout trots." This is not to make light of the disease; though most humans feel no ill effects (but become carriers), others have serious symptoms which include devastating diarrhea, and the treatment is nearly as unpleasant. The reason giardiasis has become "epidemic" is that there are more people in the backcountry—more people drinking water contaminated by animals—more people contaminating the water.

Whenever in doubt, boil the water 10 minutes. Keep in mind that *Giardia* can survive in water at or near freezing for weeks or months—a snow pond is not necessarily safe. Boiling is 100 percent effective against not only *Giardia* but the myriad other filthy little blighters that may upset your digestion or—as with some forms of hepatitis—destroy your liver.

If you cannot boil, use one of the several *iodine* treatments (chlorine compounds have been found untrustworthy in wildland circumstances), such as Potable Aqua or the more complicated method that employs iodine crystals. Rumor to the contrary, iodine treatments pose no threat to the health.

Be very wary of the filters sold in backpacking shops. One or two have been tested and found reliable (not against hepatitis) and new products are coming on the market but most filters presently available are useless or next to it.

1

McCLELLAN BUTTE

Round trip 9 miles
Hiking time 8 hours
High point 5162 feet
Elevation gain 3700 feet

Hikable July through October
One day
USGS Bandera

The sharp little peak looks formidable from Interstate 90, and because of avalanche snows in a gully it is dangerous until early July. However, a steep and rugged trail climbs to a viewpoint a few feet below the rocky summit for panoramas west over lowlands to Seattle, Puget Sound, and the Olympics, south over uncountable clearcuts to Mt. Rainier, and east to Snoqualmie Pass peaks. The lower part of the route contains numerous scars and artifacts of man's present and past activities; the recorded history of the area dates from 1853, when Captain George B. McClellan journeyed approximately this far up the valley during his search for a cross-Cascades pass for Indian fighters and immigrants. The trail is very popular even though rough in spots.

Drive Interstate 90 to Exit 42 and go off on road No. 55. Immediately beyond the Snoqualmie River bridge, turn right to the trailhead and parking lot, elevation 1500 feet.

Trail No. 1015 follows remnants of a wire-wrapped wooden water line to a bridge over Alice Creek, climbs a bit, crosses a powerline swath, enters woods again, reaches a long-abandoned, overgrown railroad grade, and at ½ mile crosses the more recently abandoned Milwaukee Railroad tracks and enters a vast clearcut. In the woods again, the trail passes mouldering mining relics and at 1 mile, 2200 feet, crosses a logging road.

Bleeding heart

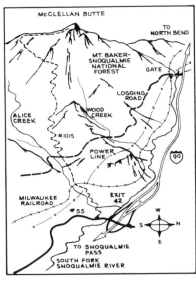

Interstate 90 from summit ridge of McClellan Butte

Find a little spring left along the road—the last sure water after July.

The way steepens, going by a sometime spring in a cool grove of large trees, then switchbacks up the wooded north face of the butte. At about 2½ miles the trail rounds the east side of the butte and crosses an avalanche gully with a treacherous snowbank that usually lasts into July. From here, with numerous switchbacks, the way sidehills below cliffs and occasional views, attaining the south ridge of the peak at 3¼ miles, 4500 feet. The trail follows the crest a short bit, with looks down into Seattle's Cedar River watershed, rounds the east side of the mountain, drops 100 feet to a small pond (possible campsites) and climbs again, passing mining garbage to a magnificent viewpoint on the ridge crest about 100 vertical feet from the summit.

The majority of hikers are content with the ridge-top view and leave the summit for experienced mountaineers; the rocks are slippery when wet, and in any conditions the exposure is sufficient to be fatal.

Tinkham road—Old: 222
             New: 55

$\underline{2}$ ANNETTE LAKE

Round trip 7¼ miles
Hiking time 4 hours
High point 3600 feet
Elevation gain 1400 feet

Hikable June through November
One day or backpack
USGS Snoqualmie Pass

A very popular and often crowded little subalpine lake, with cliffs and talus of Abiel Peak above the shores of open forest. For lonesome walking here, try early summer or late fall, in the middle of the week, in terrible weather.

Drive Interstate 90 to Exit 47. Go off the freeway and turn right .1 mile, then left on road No. 55 for .6 mile to the parking lot, elevation 2200 feet.

The way starts in an old clearcut, crosses Humpback Creek, and in 1 mile passes under a powerline and enters forest. At 1¼ miles, 2400 feet, cross the abandoned Milwaukee Railroad tracks.

Now comes the hard part, switchbacking steeply upward in nice, old forest on the slopes of Silver Peak, occasional talus openings giving looks over the valley to Humpback Mountain. After gaining 1200 feet in 1½ miles, at the 3600-foot level the way flattens out and goes along a final mile of minor ups and downs to the lake outlet, 3 miles, 3600 feet.

Wander along the east shore for picnic spots with views of small cliffs and waterfalls.

Some cross-country hikers continue to the summit of Silver Peak via the draw between Silver and Abiel Peaks, a good but quite brushy route.

Folks planning to camp do well to call the Forest Service beforehand to learn where and how they can; the lake is so mobbed that great care is being taken to avoid making it a muddy-dusty slum.

Tinkham road—Old: 222
　　　　　　 New: 55

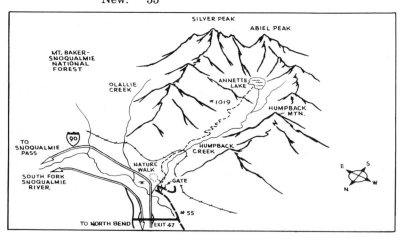

Annette Lake and cliffs of Abiel Peak

3
COLD CREEK–
SILVER PEAK LOOP

Loop trip 6 miles
Hiking time 3½ hours
High point 4200 feet
Elevation gain 1300 feet
Hikable July through October
One day
USGS Snoqualmie Pass

Sidetrip up Silver Peak 2 miles
Hiking time 2 hours
High point 5603 feet
Elevation gain 1400 feet

Grand trees, a mountain lake, and a mountaintop with great views south over rolling green ridges to Rainier, west to the Olympics (Annette Lake directly below your feet), north to Snoqualmie Pass peaks, and east across Keechelus Reservoir to Mt. Margaret, so heavily patched by clearcuts it looks as if it had a bad case of the mange.

Though much of the old beauty remains, long gone are the challenge and the remoteness that until a quarter-century ago made this one of the most popular hikes near Snoqualmie Pass. This is in the checkerboard dating from the Big Steal, the Northern Pacific Land Grant, and logging roads are built by private owners. Despite management problems the Forest Service has made a sincere effort at true multiple use—which means trails, too.

Drive Interstate 90 east from Snoqualmie Pass 2 miles and go off on Hyak Exit 54. Turn right, and right again. In .1 mile turn left on road No. 9070 and climb .4 mile to a junction. Keep straight ahead under a chairlift, ignore spur roads, and follow No. 9070 3½ miles from Interstate 90 to Cold Creek trailhead, signed "Twin Lakes," elevation 2900 feet.

(If your sole interest is the ascent of Silver, stay on No. 9070 another 2 miles to where it crosses the Pacific Crest Trail at Olallie Meadow, 4200 feet. Walk the Trail south 1½ miles to Gardiner Ridge trail, as noted below.)

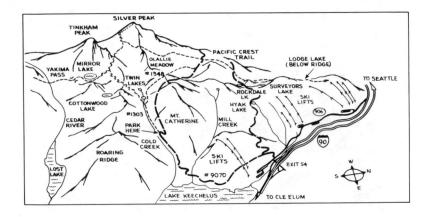

Mount Rainier from Silver Peak, Abiel Peak on right

Alternating between clearcuts and forest, Silver Peak standing 2300 feet above it all, Cold Creek trail No. 1303 attains lower Twin Lake at about ¾ mile. Here is a junction. Go either direction—the loop has as much uphill one way as the other. We describe it clockwise because that's how we happened to do it.

Cross the outlet stream and grind out 1200 feet in 1¾ miles to the Pacific Crest Trail and turn right (north). For the sidetrip ascent of Silver Peak, in an up-and-down ½ mile watch carefully for the sign marking Gardiner Ridge trail, an old route to Hanson Creek that was abandoned because part is in the Cedar River watershed. Easy to miss, the sidetrail gains 600 feet in a short ½ mile that seems a long 1 mile to heather-and-shrub parklands. The mountainside is broken by a large talus; some hikers go straight up the rocks, but skirting them left or right is easier. Above the talus follow the flowery ridge crest, then 200 feet of steep, shattered rock to the 5603-foot summit.

Returned from the sidetrip ascent to the Pacific Crest Trail, continue northward to road No. 9070 at Olallie Meadows, turn right on it about 400 feet, find trail No. 1348, and follow it 1 mile back to Twin Lakes and so home.

Old road: 2236
New road: 9070

4 SUMMIT LAKE

**Round trip to Summit Lake 5
 miles
Hiking time 3 hours
High point 5400 feet
Elevation gain 1200 feet**

**Hikable July through October
One day or backpack
USGS Enumclaw**

An alpine lake, but don't be misled by the name—it isn't on the summit of anything. However, there are flower fields and a fabulous view of Mt. Rainier.

Drive Highway 410 to a complicated intersection at the southwest corner of Buckley, turn south on Highway 162-165 for 1½ miles, and turn left on Highway 165 and proceed 18 miles, passing Wilkeson and Carbonado, following signs to Ipsut Creek and Fairfax. Just before the entrance to Mt. Rainier National Park, turn left on road No. 7810, cross the Carbon River on a wooden bridge, and drive 5.3 miles uphill to a junction with road No. 7820. Keep left on No. 7810 and at 6.9 miles reach the road-end and the trailhead, 4300 feet, to Twin Lake, Bearhead Mountain, and Summit Lake.

Going steadily east and constantly climbing, trail No. 1177 starts up through a clearcut, makes a big switchback, and enters thick forest which cuts off sights and sounds of encroaching logging and automobiles. At 1 mile, 4800 feet, is wooded Twin Lake; keep left here at the junction with Carbon trail No. 1179.

The path rounds the lake and heads uphill, passing subalpine ponds or marshes, depending on the season. Nearly at the top of the ridge the way turns west and traverses the slopes on a fairly level grade, at one point emerging from timber into a small meadow with a view of Rainier. At 2½ miles, 5400 feet, Summit Lake is attained. Bordering the shores are open fields covered with beargrass. On the west side is an old burn. The best

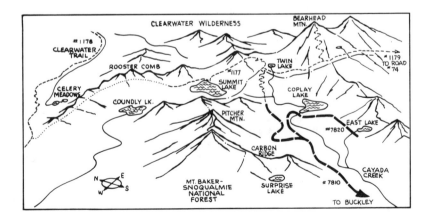

Summit Lake and Mount Rainier (John Spring photo)

camps are on the east side where the trail reaches the lake. To preserve the vegetation, hikers are asked to camp 100 feet from the shore.

For the first and most essential sidetrip, follow the trail around the lake, leave tread, find an easy route to the top of the 5737-foot hill, and look down at Coplay, Coundly, Lily, and Cedar Lakes. The view is grand of Mt. Rainier above—and equally broad of the network of logging operations below.

For an alternative or additional trip see Hike 5.

Old road: 1811
New road: 7810

Mount Rainier from lookout site on Bearhead Mountain

5 BEARHEAD MOUNTAIN

Round trip 6½ miles
Hiking time 4 hours
High point 6089 feet
Elevation gain 1800 feet

Hikable July through October
One day
USGS Enumclaw

The highest point in the new Clearwater Wilderness is an old lookout site rising above meadows that in late July and early August are the brilliant blue of lupine and red of paintbrush. Equally vivid are the miles upon miles of clearcuts to the west and the miles (or fractions thereof) of virgin forest north and east. Yet the eye is hard pressed to see all this, drawn as it is to the Great North (Willis) Wall of Mt. Rainier, avalanches impressive even at this distance—perhaps the more so because few of the monstrous masses of tumbling ice can be heard.

Drive to the Summit Lake–Bearhead trailhead (Hike 4), elevation 4300 feet.

Hike trail No. 1177 through a clearcut and up switchbacks 1 long mile to tiny Twin Lakes and a junction, 4800 feet. The left fork is to Summit Lake; go right on Carbon trail No. 1179, which contours and climbs another long mile around steep slopes to a second junction at 5400 feet on a spur ridge from the south side of the mountain. Go left ¾ mile on trail No. 1179A to the summit. Settle down and spread out your lunch. Your eyes, too, will feast.

For an alternative or additional trip see Hike 4.

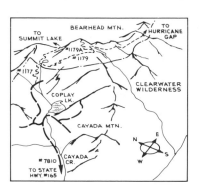

Beargrass

37

6 CLEARWATER LOOP

One-way trip 20 miles
Allow 2-3 days
High point 5250 feet

Elevation gain and loss 4300 feet
Hikable July through October
USGS Enumclaw

Surrounded on three and a half sides by clearcuts and tied to Mt. Rainier National Park on one corner, the Clearwater Wilderness is mainly marvelous old forest, prime winter habitat for wildlife, only several summits rising above treetops. Most hikers head for these high views, as described in Hikes 4 and 5. Few explore the 20-odd miles of woodland trails and creekside camps. Were it not for a 2-mile gap on a rugged, rocky ridge (old maps show a trail, never built), the trip could be a complete loop. Until a trail bypasses the ridge the "loop" requires two cars and a shuttle from trailhead to trailhead.

Drive to the Summit Lake–Bearhead Mountain trailhead (Hike 4), elevation 4300 feet, and stash a car. Backtrack in the other car to Wilkeson, and on the east end of town turn north on Railroad Avenue (probably unsigned) past the historic schoolhouse and quarry, the road now signed as No. 7710. At 5.25 miles from Highway 165 turn left on road No. 7720, drop to cross South Fork South Prairie Creek, and continue to a junction 2.5 miles from road No. 7710. Keep left on No. 7720 a long 2 miles, rounding the ridge to the valley of the East Fork, to where the big wide road switchbacks uphill. Go straight ahead on a little old road 1.25 miles, to the end of solid bottom, elevation 2750 feet. (*Note:* In 1986 new road construction will change the trailhead; check with the Forest Service.)

Find trail No. 1178, wherever, and ascend (perhaps) half-century-old second-growth and a bit of virgin forest, in a long 2 miles (1985) emerging into a 1970s clearcut at 3800 feet. The trail, flagged, follows cat tracks emanating from a Weyerhaeuser road that sometimes is open to

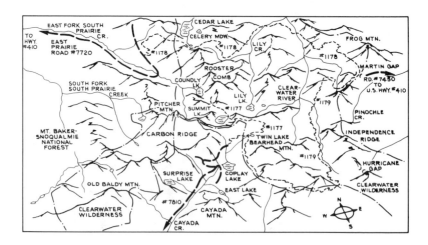

Rooster Comb Ridge from Frog Mountain

the public. (Call the Weyerhaeuser office in Snoqualmie to ask about the gate, or check with the Forest Service at the White River Ranger Station.)

Leaving the clearcut, the trail enters the Clearwater Wilderness near Celery Meadow, 4800 feet. Pass the junction with trail No. 1177 and continue on No. 1178, descending Lily Creek. Cross the creek at 2½ miles from the junction, pass a campsite at 3 miles, and at 3½ miles cross the Clearwater River, 2500 feet. The trail ascends switchbacks to road No. 7450 at Martin Gap (Hike 7), 4200 feet, 7 miles from Celery Meadow.

Head west on trail No. 1179, climbing a bit and dropping 300 feet to headwaters of the Clearwater, then climbing to Hurricane Gap, 4960 feet, 5½ miles from Martin Gap.

The trails drops 200 feet to a spectacular view of Mt. Rainier, climbs and traverses the south slopes of Bearhead Mountain, and at 8 miles from Martin Gap passes Bearhead Mountain trail No. 1179 (Hike 5), 5400 feet. The almost-loop concludes by dropping to Twin Lake and the stashed car, 10½ miles from the gap, 20 trail miles (or so) from the other car.

Old road:	194	1839	1810	1811
New road:	7710	7720	7450	7810

Mount Rainier from Frog Mountain

7 FROG MOUNTAIN

Round trip 3 miles
Hiking time 2 hours
High point 5236 feet
Elevation gain 1050 feet

Hikable July through October
One day
USGS Enumclaw

The summit gives a bird's-eye view of the virgin greenery of the Clearwater River valley and the north slopes of Bearhead Mountain and Independence Ridge and—outside the Clearwater Wilderness—countless square miles of clearcuts, some of which qualify as "tree farms," others as "timber mines." Rising huge above all is the tall, white cloud called Mt. Rainier.

Drive Highway 410 east from Enumclaw approximately 22 miles and turn off on West Fork White River road No. 74. At 6.8 miles the road crosses the river and soon starts climbing. Stay on No. 74, passing numerous well-marked sideroads. At 11.6 miles go left on road No. 7450, traversing a very steep hillside sometimes closed by rockslides. (*Note:* Its 3 miles receive limited maintenance; check with the Forest Service beforehand or be prepared for a longer day.) At 15 miles from the highway is road's end at Martin Gap, elevation 4320 feet, and the starts of Clearwater trail No. 1178, Carbon trail No. 1179, and Frog Mountain trail No. 1180.

Ascend No. 1180 from the north side of the parking lot. The way is excellent the first ¾ mile through forest to a viewpoint in a rocky little meadow, then deteriorates as the scenery enlarges. At 1¼ miles round a false summit to a saddle and a fork at the far end. The right drops 1½ miles on an unmarked trail to road No. 7450. Keep left, on the ridge, to the 5236-foot peak. Though a dozen or more trees have been cut to make way for a heliport, the views are only good to the north and east; for the complete picture pick your way to the false summit and look south and west as well.

Old road: 191   74
New road: 1810   7450

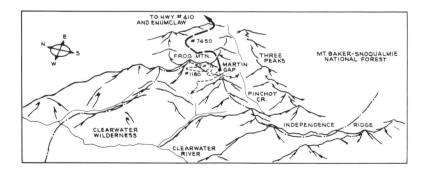

8 NACHES WAGON TRAIL

Round trip to Government Meadows from west side 10½ miles	One day or backpack USGS Lester
Hiking time 5 hours	One-way trip from east side 9½ miles
High point 4800 feet	
Elevation gain 2200 feet	Hiking time 5 hours
Hikable late June through November	High point 4900 feet
	Elevation gain 1500 feet

Walk the pioneer wagon route across Naches Pass and see blazes cut by emigrants, logs they rolled out of the way, dirt they shoveled, and trees they chopped. Unfortunately, you will see more tracks of vandals than pioneers, because the Forest Service inexcusably permits motorbikes and jeeps on the route. These adventurers seeking a mechanical challenge have obliterated much of the pioneers' trail which should have been preserved for more respectful travelers with an appreciation of history. This may be the only pioneer trail left in the lower 48 states that hasn't been paved over or bulldozed. Yet Weyerhaeuser has cut the trail with roads at four places, the Forest Service at two others, and the Forest Service has shortened the trail on the east side.

Highlights can be enjoyed in a day hike to Government Meadows from the west side, but for a better appreciation of the trek of 1853, start from the east side, camp overnight at Government Meadows (where the pioneers spent weeks), and next morning descend the west side, over "The Cliff" where wagons were lowered on rawhide ropes. In either case, allow plenty of time for leisurely exploration.

For a day hike from the west, drive Highway 410 east from Enumclaw 20 miles to a log-trestle overpass, turn left on road No. 70, and go 8 miles to the Greenwater River bridge. (*Note:* As of 1985 this bridge is washed out; check with the Forest Service or be prepared for a wade.) About .25 mile beyond, turn right on a spur road, cross Pyramid Creek, and park, elevation 2560 feet. The trail (track) takes off up the timbered ridge to the left. Ascend 3½ miles through forest to Government Meadows, 4800 feet.

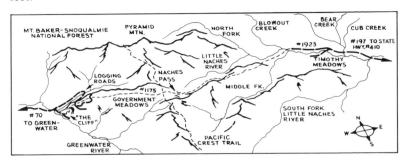

Naches Wagon Trail

For an overnight hike, leave one car at the west trailhead and drive a second over Chinook Pass and 23.5 miles east from the summit. Turn left 14 miles on Little Naches road No. 197, then turn right on road No. 1923 and go .3 mile to the trailhead, elevation 3200 feet.

The first wagon train crossed Naches Pass in 1853. One or two others followed, but the route proved so difficult it was abandoned. In 1910 the Forest Service reopened the way for foot and horse travel. To "celebrate" the centennial of the first crossing, a group of jeepsters hacked and gouged over the pass in 1953, and since then the trail has been heavily used by motorbikes and four-wheel vehicles that have rutted the forest. Thanks to the vehicles, the trail is impossible to miss, but finding remnants of the original wagon road requires imagination. Two clues are useful.

For one, the pioneers took the line of least resistance by detouring around big trees and logs; the jeepsters use chainsaws to make a more direct line, and thus in many places the old track is several hundred feet from the jeep ruts and relatively well-preserved. For a second clue, the wagons were top-heavy, and to save shoveling on sidehills the pioneers frequently followed the ups and downs of a ridge crest; particularly on the west side, jeeps have contoured around some ridge tops.

In 6 miles from the east trailhead, reach the wooded, 4900-foot summit of Naches Pass, and in another ¾ mile the Pacific Crest Trail junction and campsites at Government Meadows. The next day cross six roads on the way down; at ½ mile from the west trailhead descend "The Cliff," where pioneers lowered their wagons.

Greenwater road—Old: 197
             New: 70

9 GREENWATER RIVER– ECHO LAKE

Round trip 14 miles
Hiking time 7 hours
High point 4100 feet
Elevation gain 1640 feet

Hikable May through
  mid-November at lower
  elevations
One day or backpack
USGS Lester

Once one of the most famous cathedrals of old-growth Douglas fir outside a national park or dedicated wilderness, among the grandest valley forests in the nation, the Greenwater greenery has been whacked down and shipped overseas by loggers—though they knew full well that in several years the valley was sure to be purchased and installed in the gallery of American treasures. The Norse Peak Wilderness, which came just too late, has saved a sample, the more precious for the "free enterprise" all around. Amid the lingering big trees are sparkling forest lakes and a lovely subalpine lake.

Drive to the Naches Wagon Trail trailhead (Hike 8), elevation 2560 feet. (*Note:* As of 1985 the bridge over the Greenwater is washed out; check with the Forest Service or be prepared to wade.)

Follow Greenwater trail No. 1176 to the clearcut edge and enter a magnificence of old trees thrusting high above a rich understory of devil's club, vanilla leaf, trillium, and moss—much, much moss. (Yet just a short way up the steep valley walls on either side is loggers' "daylight," and from it the storm waters formerly held back by forest are carrying gravel and boulders and logging slash down to the river.)

At ¾ mile the trail crosses Greenwater River, a limeade joy, and at 1½ miles recrosses at the first of the two little Meeker (Greenwater) Lakes. The second is at 2 miles. At 4 miles the trail reaches a junction with Lost Creek trail No. 1185, a 3-mile sidetrip to Lost Lake. So far the trail has gained only 200 feet a mile, but near the 5-mile mark it leaves the valley

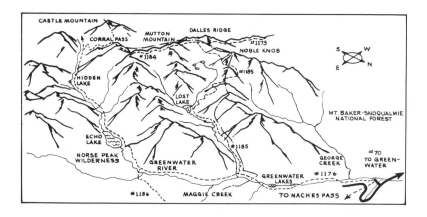

Greenwater River crossing

bottom and starts climbing in earnest. At 5½ miles pass a junction with trail No. 1186. At 6½ miles cross a 4100-foot high point and drop 300 feet to the edge of 3819-foot Echo Lake, surrounded by wooded hills with a glimpse of meadows and craggy peaks of Castle Mountain.

The trail continues 6 miles to Corral Pass. The entire route, near lakes and along river, offers numerous campsites. At Echo Lake campers are asked to keep 100 feet from the water; the west shore is closed.

Old road: 197
New road: 70

10 NOBLE KNOB

Round trip to Noble Knob 7 miles
Hiking time 5 hours
High point 6011 feet
Elevation gain 900 feet in, 600 feet out

Hikable July through October
One day or backpack
USGS Lester

Round trip to George Lake 9 miles

If you want flowers, burn up the trees. As the result of a fire set by lightning (or somebody) in the 1920s, the fields of color here rival those of Paradise. In stark contrast to the at-hand yellows and blues and reds is the whiteness of the north side of Mt. Rainier, not far away across the valley, close enough to see crevasses in the Emmons Glacier and cinders of the crater rim.

The trail lies along the edge of Norse Peak Wilderness, occasionally dipping into the preserve, meaning at least part of the trail will be free from machines. Note the extensive rehabilitation work done by the Forest Service in meadows ravaged by jeepsters and cyclists—destroyers that should not have been allowed in the first place.

Drive Highway 410 east 30 miles from the White River Ranger Station in Enumclaw to just 1.5 miles short of Mt. Rainier National Park and turn up road No. 7174, signed "Corral Pass Campground." Ascend this very steep road 5.8 miles to Noble Knob trail No. 1184, elevation 5100 feet.

The trail contours a steep hillside, alternating ¾ mile between flowers and groves of subalpine trees, and then follows the now-abandoned jeep road another ¾ mile. A short, steep bit concludes with a resumption of trail. At 2 miles pass Deep Creek trail, and at 2½ miles reach a 6000-foot saddle. The trail now drops steadily. At 3 miles, directly above Twentyeight Mile Lake, pass Dalles Ridge trail No. 1173. Shortly beyond, at 5600 feet, is a three-way junction.

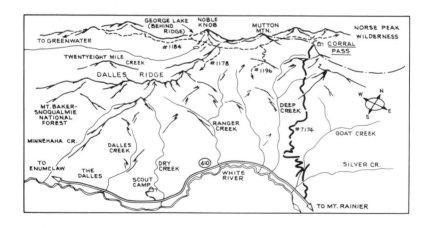

The left fork descends past George Lake (a mile from the junction a sidepath contours right to the lake, 5500 feet, and campsites) to road No. 196. The right fork goes down past Lost Lake to the Greenwater trail (Hike 9). Take the middle trail, cross a large meadow, and with one switchback in a path overgrown in blossoms, traverse completely around the mountain to the old lookout site atop Noble Knob.

Old road: 185
New road: 7174

Fog-shrouded Noble Knob trail

Crystal Mountain ski area from Norse Peak

WHITE RIVER
Norse Peak Wilderness

11   BIG CROW BASIN— NORSE PEAK

Round trip to Norse Peak 8½ miles
Hiking time 6 hours
High point 6856 feet
Elevation gain 2900 feet

Hikable late June through early November
One day
USGS Bumping Lake

Lovely alpine meadows, one with a small lake, offering a wonderful weekend of wandering. However, the shortest way to the basin involves climbing nearly to the top of 6856-foot Norse Peak—an arduous backpack. Most hikers therefore settle for a day trip to the summit, an abandoned lookout site, and enjoy the views down to the inviting gardens and all around to panoramas extending from Snoqualmie Pass peaks to Mt. Adams, from golden hills of Eastern Washington to green lowlands of Puget Sound. The trail to Norse Peak usually is open for walking in late

June; the meadow country remains under snow until mid-July.

Drive Highway 410 east 33 miles from Enumclaw to Silver Springs summer homes. A bit beyond, just before the Rainier National Park boundary, turn left toward the Crystal Mountain ski area. At 4 miles, 3900 feet, park.

Find the old mine-to-market road, No. (7190)410, walk it about 1000 feet, and go off left on trail No. 1191. The original path to the lookout was short and steep; the Forest Service recently improved the route, which now is somewhat gentler but considerably longer.

Very soon the tip of Mt. Rainier appears over the ridge to the west and every additional step reveals more of the mountain. By 2 miles the whole summit is in sight and the scene steadily expands as more elevation is gained. The route is confused here and there by crisscrossing of the old tread—take the path of least resistance, which generally is the new trail. At 4 miles, 6600 feet, the summit ridge is topped and a junction reached.

The right fork follows the ridge crest ¼ mile to Norse Peak. Look northeast into Big Crow Basin and east to Lake Basin and appealing Basin Lake. Look down to the Crystal Mountain ski area, one of the finest ski developments in the Northwest; unfortunately, winter doesn't last all year and the summer view is a hodgepodge of bulldozer tracks.

The left fork drops eastward 1 mile to join the Pacific Crest Trail, which descends ½ mile to Big Crow Basin; at about 5700 feet are a shelter cabin and good camping, though water may be scarce in late summer. Partway down find a sidetrail leading over a low green ridge to Basin Lake, 6200 feet.

The meadows and peak also can be approached by intersecting the Crest Trail at Bullion Basin or by taking the trail starting at Corral Pass, 5600 feet. The latter long and scenic route includes two descents and ascents of 800 feet each in 4 miles before joining the Crest Trail near Little Crow Basin (camps and water).

Old road: 184
New road: (7190)410

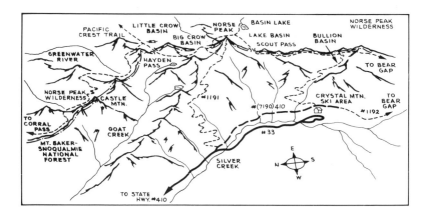

12 CRYSTAL MOUNTAIN LOOP

Round trip to viewpoint 6 miles
Hiking time 3½ hours
High point 5500 feet
Elevation gain 1300 feet
Hikable July through September
One day
USGS Bumping Lake and White
  River Park

Loop trip 13 miles
Hiking time 7 hours
High point 6776 feet
Elevation gain 2400 feet

Along the Crystal Mountain Trail, boundary of Mt. Rainier National
Park, a Forest Service trail wanders through a series of striking views of
Rainier and the White River. Flowers in one season, great huckleberries
in another. Hikers who get up early enough in the morning have a good
chance of seeing elk.

The trip comes in two versions, one using the feet only for a standard
uphill-downhill walk, the other using the Crystal Mountain chairlift for
the uphill, a trail-road combination for the downhill. Both will be described here, the "normal" version first.

From Highway 410 at the park boundary near Silver Springs, turn left
on the Crystal Mountain Highway. Drive 4.5 miles to road No. (7190)410
on the right and follow it .25 mile to the trailhead and horse-unloading
ramp, elevation 4200 feet.

Trail No. 1163 begins as a service road under a powerline but soon becomes legitimate, climbing gently through clearcuts, then an old burn, in
loose, dusty, pumice soil. Shade is scarce and water nonexistent. (Did you
remember to fill the canteen?) Heat and thirst are forgotten when, in 3
miles, at 5500 feet, the crest of Crystal Mountain is attained and Mt.
Rainier overpowers the horizon.

The ridge varies from narrow, with a cliff on the park side, to broad
and rounded meadows. Below the crest are vast fields of huckleberries.
And the views! Chances are a party will find ample rewards long before
completing the 3 steady-climbing ridge-crest miles to the top terminal of
Chair No. 2.

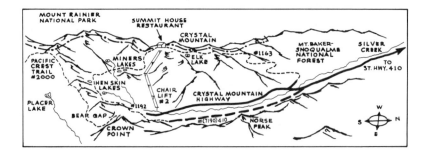

White River and Mount Rainier from Crystal Ridge

For a loop trip with an interesting variety of lakes, meadows, and huckleberries, descend on a service road that starts near the terminal. In ⅓ mile find a legitimate trail switchbacking down through Silver Queen Basin, past Hen Skin Lakes, to a junction with Silver Creek trail No. 1192. Follow it 1 mile to road No. (7190)410, then go by road to the ski area parking lot, 4½ miles from the top terminal. From there walk the paved road 2½ miles back to the starting point; alternately, follow the old mine road, No. (7190)410, to Crystal Mountain Highway, cross, and return on the trail.

Now for the all-downhill tour. (Let it be noted this version is no good for elk watching—by the time of day the chairlifts start running, the animals have finished eating and retired to the forest to chew their cuds.) Drive to the ski area parking lot, elevation 4200 feet, ride Chair No. 2 to the top, elevation 6776 feet, and find the Crystal Ridge trail and hike either way. Both ways are so interesting and different that you may want to go back a second time for the other direction or, as we did, start early in the morning so you can see the elk and hike the whole loop at one time.

Old road: 184
New road: (7190)410

Sheep Lake

AMERICAN RIVER
Norse Peak Wilderness

13   SOURDOUGH GAP

Round trip 6 miles
Hiking time 4 hours
High point 6400 feet
Elevation gain 1100 feet in, 200
    feet out

Hikable July through October
One day or backpack
USGS Mt. Rainier and Bumping
    Lake

A delightful bit of the Pacific Crest Trail (probably the easiest meadow walk in this entire book) through flower gardens and grassy fields to a high pass. A good overnight hike for beginners, except that camping space is limited and very crowded on weekends. Do the trip in early August when flowers are at their peak.

Drive Highway 410 east from Enumclaw to the summit of Chinook Pass, 5432 feet. Find the first available parking lot—which may be around the bend in the highway. (The shortage of parking space is a serious problem on fine summer weekends. So is the vandalism of cars left overnight.) The trailhead (Pacific Crest Trail No. 2000) is near the wooden overpass.

The trail goes north, paralleling the highway, dropping slightly in the first mile, at times on cliffs almost directly above the road. At about 1½ miles the way rounds a ridge, leaves the highway, and starts a gentle climb to Sheep Lake, 2½ miles, 5700 feet—a great place to camp if not crowded. But it almost always is, and the meadows have been badly damaged. Find better camping on benches a few hundred feet away.

The moderate ascent continues through flowers, with a final long switchback leading to Sourdough Gap, 3 miles, 6400 feet. (About 500 feet below the gap the summit of Mt. Rainier can be seen briefly between two peaks to the west.)

Views from the gap are limited. For broader vistas, continue on the trail another ⅓ mile, descending a little to a small pass with looks down Morse Creek to Placer Lake, an artificial lake made by miners years ago.

For really wide horizons, ascend the 6734-foot peak west of the gap— not a difficult climb by mountaineering standards, but steep with a loose scree slope near the top. Drop a few feet north from the gap and start up along the base of cliffs, following a well-worn path. For the best footing stay off the scree. From the summit admire the huge white bulk of Mt. Rainier, peaks south to Mt. Adams, and north along the Cascade Crest. A vertical cliff falls to Crystal Lakes 900 feet below, seemingly only a swan dive away.

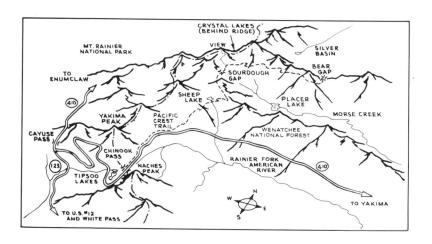

14 UNION CREEK

Round trip 8 miles
Hiking time 4 hours
High point 4500 feet
**Elevation gain 1300 feet in, 400
feet out**

**Hikable late June through
October**
One day or backpack
USGS Bumping Lake

A pleasant valley walk through forests by a mountain stream is high-lighted by superb falls. The woodland camps beside the waters where the ouzels dip-dip-dip are more comfortable from July on, when the snow has melted and the meltwater dried up.

From Chinook Pass drive Highway 410 east, passing Lodgepole Campground at 7.4 miles; at 9.2 miles, just before the highway crosses Union Creek, turn left on an unsigned forest road a few hundred feet to the start of trail No. 956, elevation 3500 feet. (From Yakima drive High-way 410 west 9.7 miles from Bumping River junction to Union Creek.)

In ¼ mile look up Union Creek to a large waterfall. After the trail crosses the creek and commences switchbacks, two spurs drop to the falls, both worth investigating, the second the more exciting. The trail climbs 600 feet in the first mile, often steeply, then goes up and down to another fine falls on North Fork Union Creek, crossed on a bridge at the falls' top. Downhill some and uphill more, the way ascends to 4500 feet, then loses altitude to the creek level and campsites above and below the 4-mile marker, 4250 feet.

The trail follows the creek closely almost ½ mile before beginning a long, steep uphill to Cement Basin trail No. 987 at 6½ miles and the Pacific Crest Trail at 7 miles, near Bluebell Pass and remains of the old Bluebell Mine.

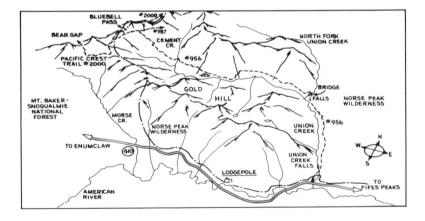

Crossing North Fork Union Creek

15   CROW LAKE WAY

Round trip to Grassy Saddle 10 miles
Hiking time 8 hours
High point 6200 feet
Elevation gain 3000 feet in, 600 feet out

Hikable early June to hunting season
One day or backpack
USGS Bumping Lake

A steep trail, with no water except that carried in canteens, climbs from valley forests to high meadows, compensating for the sweat and struggle by offering exciting views of the needlelike spires of Fifes Peaks and the meandering course of the American River. The route can be continued past pretty little Grassy Saddle to the large, boggy meadows surrounding Crow Creek Lake, a favorite haunt of throngs of elk and deer. The animals are fun to watch in the summer but are best steered clear of in that season when hunters outnumber the huntees.

Drive Highway 410 east of Chinook Pass to 1.2 miles east of Pleasant Valley Campground and find the trailhead, elevation 3400 feet.

Crow Lake Way No. 953 commences with a long, steady uphill haul, gaining 2200 feet in 3½ miles. The trail begins by entering Norse Peak Wilderness, several hundred feet from the highway. Switchbacks climb 2¼ miles through forest to a hogback, which then is followed (with glimpses of Fifes Peaks) past dramatic drop-offs overlooking American Ridge, the views growing step by step, to a 5800-foot high point at 4 miles, a good turnaround for day trippers.

The trail descends 200 feet into Survey Creek drainage and at 4½ miles crosses a broad divide, 6000 feet, to Crow Creek drainage. West are rolling green meadows inviting a tour. At about 5 miles, 5600 feet, the trail enters Grassy Saddle with a small creek and, half hidden in trees, a very small lake. Campsites nearby are great bases for explorations.

For the first, roam the basin at the head of Falls Creek. The unmarked trail starts at the far end of the lake, skirts a rockslide, and climbs to the

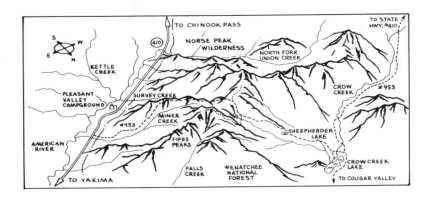

Fifes Peaks from Crow Lake Way

basin edge at 6400 feet. The basin rim can be followed like the lip of a cup in a semicircle to cliffs of Fifes Peaks. Other explorations are the 6400-foot hill to the west and, longer, the 3 miles along Crow Lake Way, in green meadows, to Crow Creek Lake.

Fifes Peaks from Fifes Ridge trail

16   FIFES RIDGE

**Round trip to Fifes Ridge
  viewpoint 10 miles
Hiking time 8 hours
High point 6315 feet
Elevation gain 3000 feet**

**Hikable May through October
One day or backpack
USGS Bumping Lake**

Overlook the spectacular cliffs and pinnacles of Fifes Peaks. Gaze around the horizon to Rainier, Stuart, Adams, and Goat Rocks. Direct your eyes past the tips of your toes, down to silvery wanderings of the American River, where you came from. Lift your eyes to American Ridge, across the valley in the companion William O. Douglas Wilderness.

From Chinook Pass drive Highway 410 east 13.5 miles, 2.6 miles beyond Pleasant Valley Campground, and find the trailhead parking area on the uphill side of the highway near Wash Creek, elevation 3320 feet. (From Yakima drive Highway 410 west 2.5 miles beyond the Bumping Lake junction, .7 mile beyond Hells Crossing Campground.)

Fifes Ridge trail No. 954 climbs moderately along the west bank of Wash Creek about 1 mile, takes a deep breath, and tilts the angle to gain 1800 feet in the next 2 miles—fortunately, in forest shade. At 1½ miles Wash Creek is crossed and at 2 miles recrossed; this is the last water on the summit route.

At 2¾ miles the trail tops Fifes Ridge and comes to an unmarked junction. If your trip is an overnight backpack, go straight ahead, descending 300 feet and contouring to camps along Falls Creek. For the high views turn right and continue up, at 3 miles gaining a 5400-foot bare knoll and first views of the dramatic south face of Fifes Peaks. Fill your eyes but continue 2 miles, up and down Fifes Ridge, to a 6300-foot knoll and the climax panoramas.

Old maps show a trail completely around Fifes Peaks. Don't believe it. Whatever path may have existed earlier in the century has long since vanished.

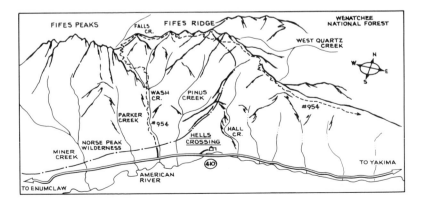

17 MESATCHEE CREEK TO COUGAR LAKES

Round trip 22 miles
Allow 2–3 days
High point 6000 feet
Elevation gain 2900 feet in, 1400
feet out

Hikable mid-July through
September
USGS Bumping Lake

The hiking distance to Cougar Lakes is longer by this approach than from the Bumping River (Hike 20). However, it avoids the ford of the Bumping, not always a lead-pipe cinch. Anyway, the ascent up the creek valley is a proper joy, and the ramble along American Ridge (Hike 18) is the most fun of the whole trip.

Drive Highway 410 east from Chinook Pass 6.5 miles and turn right .4 mile on road No. (1700)460 to Mesatchee Creek trail No. 969, elevation 3600 feet.

The first 1¼ level miles lie along an old road, perhaps partly the original miner's road to Morse Creek. Cross American River on a log, enter William O. Douglas Wilderness, and in 1½ miles intersect Dewey Lake trail No. 968. Go left, remaining on No. 969, which gets down to business, switchbacking upward. Mesatchee Creek now can be heard, then comes a waterfall and the first view of the creek. At 2½ miles the way moderates and at 3¾ miles, 4900 feet, crosses the creek to an excellent camp.

The trail traverses a 1929 burn, now become a miniaturized forest of little subalpine fir and western larch Christmas trees. At 4½ miles cross a small stream with limited camping and at 5½ miles join American Ridge trail No. 958, 5850 feet.

It's not compulsory to head for Cougar Lakes—the ridge itself is an excellent destination. Go east a few hundred yards to a knoll with views of Bumping Lake, Mt. Adams, the rugged summits of House Rock, Crag

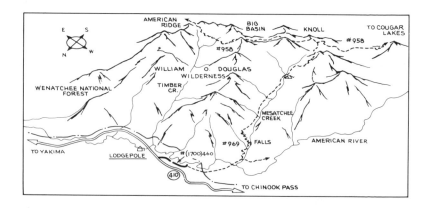

Waterfall on Mesatchee Creek

Mountain, Mt. Aix, and Bismark Peak, and the more rounded Nelson Ridge and Tumac Mountain.

For Cougar Lakes turn west, losing 300 feet, switchbacking up 500 feet over a green meadow to a 6000-foot high point, and descending again, at 9½ miles intersecting Swamp Creek trail No. 970, 5000 feet. Keep straight ahead, shortly passing the American Lake trail and coming to Cougar Lakes, 11 miles, 5015 feet.

Old road: 1710
New road: (1700)460

18   AMERICAN RIDGE

Round trip from Goose Prairie to
  viewpoint 12 miles
Hiking time 7 hours
High point 6310 feet
Elevation gain 2900 feet
Hikable June through November
One day or backpack
USGS Bumping Lake

One-way trip from Goose Prairie
  to Pacific Crest Trail 19 miles
Allow 3 days
High point 6946 feet
Elevation gain 5500 feet
Hikable late July through
  October

As the crow flies, American Ridge is 17 miles long, but with twists, turns, and switchbacks, the trail takes 27 miles to complete the traverse. The way is mostly rough and sometimes steep, but the meadowlands are beautiful and lonesome. Flowers are in full bloom at the east end of the ridge about Memorial Day (the usual time that Chinook Pass opens) and at the west end in early August. The east end makes an excellent early-season trip when other high trails are still snowed in. Look for avalanche and glacier lilies and a rare pink-and-purple flower called steer's head.

The entire ridge is worth hiking, but only the east end is free of snow in June, and by August it is dry and hot. Therefore the recommendation is to hike from Goose Prairie to an intersection with the American Ridge trail and then go east (in June) or west (in August) along the ridge crest.

Drive Highway 410 east from Chinook Pass 19 miles and turn right on the Bumping River road. In .6 mile is the eastern trailhead, elevation 2900 feet, signed "American Ridge trail No. 958"; if a complete traverse of American Ridge is planned, start here.

At 9.3 miles from Highway 410 find Goose Prairie trail No. 972 on the right side of the road, elevation 3360 feet. Parking space in a small camp on the left.

The Goose Prairie trail is in woods all the way, beginning in fir and pine forest typical of the east slopes of the Cascades and ascending into Alaska cedars, alpine firs, and wind-bent pines. The route climbs steadily but never steeply. At 1½ miles the path crosses several small streams

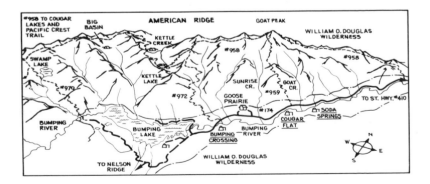

View from American Ridge trail

and begins a series of nine switchbacks, at 2 miles recrossing the same streams. At 4¾ miles is a spring that runs most of the summer; possible camping here. At 5 miles the ridge top is attained and so is the intersection with American Ridge trail No. 958, elevation 6200 feet.

Day hikers (any season) should follow the ridge west, climbing ½ mile to a point where the trail starts down into Kettle Creek drainage. Leave the trail and continue ¼ mile more up the ridge to a 6310-foot knoll with fine views of Mt. Rainier, Mt. Aix, and miles of ridges north and south.

Early-season overnight hikers should turn east, following the ridge through forest and meadows to Goat Peak at 11 miles, site of the former American Ridge Lookout, elevation 6473 feet, and a view of the spectacular cliffs of Fifes Peaks. If transportation has been arranged, a party can continue 7½ miles down to the Bumping River road and the previously mentioned American Ridge trailhead, completing a one-way trip of 18½ miles with an elevation gain of about 3600 feet.

Midsummer and fall overnight hikers should turn west, climbing near the top of the 6310-foot knoll, then descending to campsites at shallow Kettle Lake, 6 miles, 5650 feet. (Below the lake is a small spring.) The trail contours around the head of Kettle Creek, climbing to the ridge crest at 10 miles, 6946 feet, dropping again to Big Basin at 11 miles, 6300 feet, a cirque with good campsites, bands of elk, and glorious scenery.

With some ups and more downs, the trail follows the ridge top from meadows back into alpine forest at a low point of 5500 feet, then up to meadowland at 6000 feet and a campsite near Mud Lake at 13½ miles. At 16½ miles is a junction with Swamp Lake trail No. 970, a popular route leading to Cougar Lakes in 1 mile and a steep way trail that joins the Crest Trail; No. 958 goes right, reaching American Lake at 18 miles and the Crest Trail at 19½ miles.

If transportation can be arranged, a one-way trip can be made via the Crest Trail to Chinook Pass, a total distance of 26.5 miles, or via the Swamp Lake trail to Upper Bumping road, a total of 21 miles.

Mount Rainier from Goat Peak on American Ridge

GOAT PEAK

Round trip 10 miles
Hiking time 6 hours
High point 6473 feet
Elevation gain 3400 feet

Hikable late June through
October
One day
USGS Bumping Lake and Old
Scab Mountain

A former lookout site on the highest summit of 17-mile-long American Ridge gives views down to the American River, north across the valley to impressive cliffs of Fifes Peaks, south over Bumping Reservoir to Aix and Adams, and west over Chinook Pass to Rainier. The peak is a quick sidetrip for hikers on the American Ridge trail (Hike 18), but that's a journey of a number of days; the shortest approach from the road is described here. The trail is dry, so carry water; for camping go early in summer when snowmelt rills are running.

Drive Highway 410 east 19 miles from Chinook Pass and turn right on Bumping River road 5.7 miles to Goat Creek trail No. 959, elevation 3100 feet.

The trail, never near the creek for which it is named, briskly climbs steep forest slopes in long and short switchbacks, in 4 strenuous miles intersecting American Ridge trail No. 958. A short distance from the ridge top the views begin.

Go north on the ridge 1 mile to a short spur that climbs 300 feet to the summit, 6473 feet. By use of a second car the return to Bumping River road can be made by either trail No. 958 or No. 972 (Hike 18).

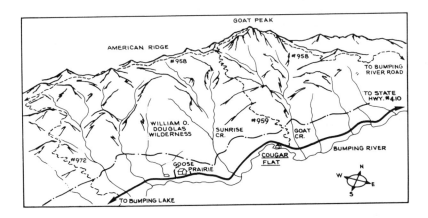

20 COUGAR LAKES

Round trip to Cougar Lakes 12 miles
Hiking time 8 hours
High point 5300 feet
Elevation gain 1700 feet in, 300 feet out

Hikable mid-July through October
One day or backpack
USGS Bumping Lake

Two alpine lakes, a big one and a little one, surrounded by generous flower fields in late July and early August, blueberries in early September, and fall colors in October. From ridges above, wide views of Mt. Rainier and the Cascade Crest country. Bumping River must be forded on this approach, not too difficult in midsummer when the river is low, but when the water is high, Mesatchee Creek trail (Hike 17) may be a better alternative.

Drive Highway 410 east from Chinook Pass 19 miles and turn right 10.8 miles on the Bumping River road to the end of pavement at Bumping Lake. Continue on road No. 200 to a junction at 2.5 miles and turn right on the Upper Bumping road 3.6 miles to the road-end and trailhead, elevation 3600 feet.

The flat forest way leads in ½ mile to a ford of the broad and shallow Bumping River, which has very cold water and sharp rocks, so wear wool socks or tennis shoes—or boots without socks, which thus are kept dry for redonning. A bit farther is a junction with the Bumping Lake trail. Go straight ahead, climbing moderately and steadily in woods and occasional openings to the outlet of Swamp Lake, almost 3¾ miles, 4800 feet; campsites at and near the shelter cabin.

The trail ascends several hundred feet in ¾ mile to an indistinct divide and a junction with the American Ridge trail (Hike 18). Go left ¼ mile to another junction. The right-hand trail climbs past American Lake to the

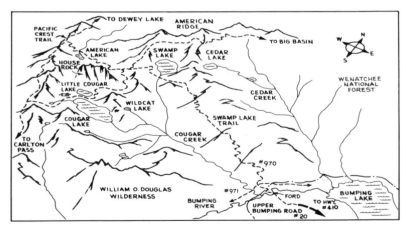

Little Cougar Lake and House Rock

Pacific Crest; go left instead, rounding a ridge spur at 5300 feet and dropping into the lake basin, at 6 miles, 5015 feet, reaching the isthmus between the Cougar Lakes.

To the right is Little Cougar Lake, at the foot of the basalt cliffs of House Rock. To the left is Big Cougar Lake. The shores offer numerous camps but the sites with the most privacy and largest views are in meadows along the inlet stream feeding Big Cougar Lake. (Be sure to camp a distance from lakeshore and streams.)

For extended horizons, climb a steep and perhaps very muddy mile on the boulder-strewn path leading from the inlet of Big Cougar to the Pacific Crest at 6000 feet. Look for mountain goat, marmots, and rock conies (pikas). For maximum scenery and garden walking, wander north on the Pacific Crest Trail and in about 1½ miles turn right on the trail down to American Lake and back to Cougar Lakes, completing a 5-mile loop.

To preserve the vegetation, camp at least 100 feet from the lakeshores and—whenever possible—200 feet from the Pacific Crest Trail.

Old road: 174
New road: 200

21 BUMPING RIVER

Round trip 16 miles
Allow 2 days
High point 4200 feet
Elevation gain 500 feet, plus many ups and downs
Hikable August through September
USGS Bumping Lake

A very easy (except for one bit) forest trail ascends the meandering Bumping River through a valley that is a year-round home of deer and a band of elk, often seen by quiet hikers, and finally rises to the river's

Bumping River

source on the Cascade Crest. The walk is magnificent in late June and early July when wildflowers are blooming in the woods. However, that noneasy bit—the ford of the Bumping River—is then downright dangerous, and thus the recommendation to wait for the snowmelt to run low.

Drive Highway 410 east from Chinook Pass 19 miles and turn right on the Bumping River road 13.3 miles. Turn right on road No. 200 and in 2.5 miles find Fish Lake Way No. 971A, elevation 3700 feet.

The first 1¾ miles climb a bit and drop some 360 feet to the Bumping River. This much can be hiked in the time of forest flowering without difficulty. However, the horse ford never is absolutely a breeze for pedestrians and until a certain time in summer is a horror. If a person dislikes the look of it, he can bushwhack upstream to see if, by chance, a footlog is available. The final alternative is to return to the trailhead and go somewhere else, such as to Twin Sisters Lakes and Tumac Mountain (Hike 23).

Once across the river the trail is a pussycat. At 2 miles it intersects trail No. 971, at 4½ miles crosses Red Rock Creek on a log to a pair of nice camps, and at 5½ miles passes a small, nameless lake. The Pacific Crest Trail is attained at 7¾ miles, and in a final ¼ mile, Fish Lake, 4200 feet, shallow and swampy, but with possible campsites.

Before starting home, be sure to sidetrip north on the Crest Trail, climbing 1200 feet to steep and luscious alpine meadows with broad views of volcanoes, active and dormant.

Old road: 174
New road: 200

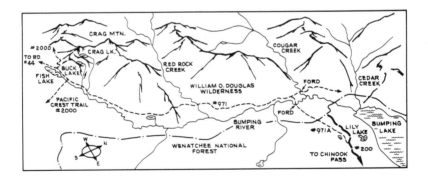

22
NELSON RIDGE—
MOUNT AIX

Round trip to Mt. Aix 12 miles
Hiking time 10 hours
High point 7766 feet
Elevation gain 4000 feet

Hikable mid-June through
  September
One day
USGS Bumping Lake

High gardens in the blue sky of the rainshadow, featuring views east to the brown vastness of the heat-hazy Columbia Plateau, west to the shimmering white hugeness of Mt. Rainier, and south along the Cascade Crest to the Goat Rocks and Mt. Adams. Plus closer looks over meadows and forests of the William O. Douglas Wilderness. This is not a beginner's trail—the way is steep, hot, and dry.

Drive Highway 410 east from Chinook Pass 19 miles and turn right on the Bumping River road 11 miles to a junction. Take the left fork, road No. 20080, 1.5 miles and just before a bridge over Copper Creek turn left up a steep road signed, "Mt. Aix Trail." Park in a few yards, elevation 3700 feet. The climb on trail No. 982 is dry and long to the last spring at 3½ miles, so carry water.

The merciless trail attains highlands with minimum delay. For openers, the path ascends deep forest nearly to a branch of Cooper Creek but never gets to the water, instead switchbacking up a steep hillside. (Across the Copper Creek valley, above Miners Ridge, Rainier appears, and grows with every step.) At 2¼ miles the trail swings into open subalpine forest at the lip of a hanging valley but again never gets to water. Switchbacks now trend out from the valley into open forest distinguished by superb specimens of whitebark pine.

At 3½ miles is that (last) spring, with a small but cozy campsite, more than acceptable when the way beyond is under snow. At nearly 4 miles, 6400 feet, is a grassy promontory with views of Rainier, Adams, and the

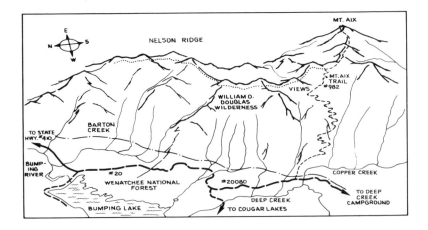

Looking south along Nelson Ridge

Goat Rocks—a nice campsite here in early summer, after snowbanks have melted partly away and while snowmelt still is available. This far makes a satisfying destination for a day hike, especially when slopes above are snowy or the party is pooped.

From the promontory the trail traverses shrubby forest and scree southward and upward to the wide-open crest of Nelson Ridge, 7100 feet, and a choice of wanderings. The up-and-down crest cries out for rambling in either or both directions. The trail contours and climbs a final rocky mile to the summit of 7766-foot Mt. Aix, one-time site of a fire lookout.

Because of their position on the east slope of the Cascades, and the mostly southwest exposures of the trail route, Nelson Ridge and Mt. Aix are free of snow weeks earlier than country a few miles distant. And if the tread at the hanging valley of Copper Creek is all white, as it may be through June, a short and simple detour up amid trees leads back to clear ground. Actually, the maximum flower display comes when patches of snow still linger. The locals consider this trail—whether to the promontory at 4 miles, to Nelson Ridge at 5 miles, or Mt. Aix at 6 miles—the best early-summer hike in the entire Bumping River area.

Old road: 162
New road: 20080

23 TUMAC MOUNTAIN— TWIN SISTERS LAKES

Round trip 10½ miles
Hiking time 5 hours
High point 6340 feet
Elevation gain 2100 feet

Hikable July through October
One day or backpack
USGS Bumping Lake and White
Pass

Hike through alpine meadows by myriad lakes and ponds to the most varied view of vulcanism in the Washington Cascades. Tumac itself—postglacial, and probably younger than 10,000 years—is no simple cone but rather built of both cinders and lava and having two craters (both lake-filled), an infant stratovolcano standing on a broad lava plateau. This is how mighty Rainier began. The summit presents a panorama of stratovolcanoes of other ages: Spiral Butte, another infant, at the south end of the lava plateau; youthful St. Helens, expected by geologists to grow and violently blow a lot more; bulky, mature, deeply dissected Rainier and Adams; and the old, old Goat Rocks, remnant of a once-mighty volcano now reduced to mere roots. Do the climb in mid-July when upper slopes are covered with red and white heather plus a peppering of bright red paintbrush. The trip can be one day or overnight, camping at one of the lovely Twin Sisters Lakes. Carry water; except for the lakes, the way can be quite dry.

Drive Highway 410 east from Chinook Pass 19 miles and turn right 10.8 miles on the Bumping River road to the end of pavement at Bumping Lake. Continue on road No. 200 to a junction at 2.5 miles and turn left on road No. 20080, going 7 miles to the road-end at Deep Creek Campground, elevation 4300 feet.

Find Twin Sisters trail No. 980 on the north side of the campground. The way gains 800 feet in 2¼ miles (all in woods) to Little Twin Sister Lake, 5100 feet.

The "little" lake (only a comparison; both are quite large) has numer-

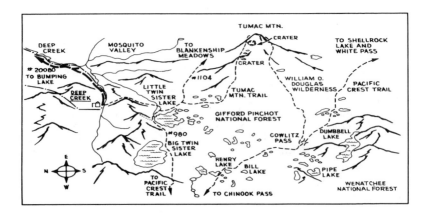

Beargrass on top of Tumac Mountain

ous bays and rocky points. To see it at its best, climb open slopes of the 5733-foot hill rising above the shores. To reach Big Twin Sister Lake, follow trail No. 980 westward ½ mile. Both lakes are outstanding and have beautiful campsites. They have many delightful sand beaches, the more so since the replenishment of May 18, 1980.

From Little Twin Sister Lake turn left on trail No. 1104, which in ½ mile turns toward Blankenship Meadows. Keep straight ahead on Tumac Mountain trail No. 44, which aims at the peak. The way climbs steadily in open meadows 1 mile. Note how small trees are taking over the meadowland, a phenomenon that only recently has received attention. Are the trees just now growing after the Ice Age, or are they returning after catastrophic forest fires, insect invasion, or uncontrolled stock grazing of years ago? Whatever the reason, alpine meadows all over this portion of the Cascades are rapidly changing to forest, especially here and at Mt. Rainier.

The final mile is steep and badly chewed up by horses, but the views get steadily better and become downright exciting on the 6340-foot summit. The most striking is northeast, down to Blankenship Meadows and the three Blankenship Lakes (Hike 27). To the west are many tree-ringed lakes, a few of which can be seen, including Dumbbell Lake (Hike 29). Mt. Aix and neighbors dominate the northeast horizon. In other directions are the volcanoes.

To protect the vegetation, campers are asked to use sites at least 100 feet from the lakeshores. At Big Twin Sister, most of the permitted camps are on the south side, one on the north.

Incidentally, don't try to puzzle out an Indian source for "Tumac." Two "Macs," probably McAllister and McCall, grazed sheep in the area.

Old road: 174 162
New road: 200 20080

24 RATTLESNAKE MEADOWS

Round trip 20 miles
Allow 2–3 days
High point 3800 feet
Elevation gain 600 feet, plus many
  ups and downs

Hikable August and September
USGS Meeks Table, Timberwolf
  Mountain, Rimrock Lake, White
  Pass

The William O. Douglas Wilderness has a split personality: the misty-lush Pacific Crest and the rainshadow east, where desert plants mingle with subalpine, the sun shines (almost) all the time, and (yes) there are (a few) rattlesnakes. The quintessence of the east is the Rattlesnake, and a person easily could spend a week ascending the stream to its source, exploring sidetrails to 7000-foot peaks. For a hiker the objections to the trail are two: the first 2-odd miles are on a jeepers' "trail" (their exclusion *must* be arranged); even so, this stretch would be a delightful early-summer walk except that at 3 miles is the first of 14 fords, ruling out the trip for the average pedestrian until the low water of August.

Drive Highway 410 east from Chinook Pass about 36 miles, pass the first of two "Nile Roads," and at about 39 miles turn right on the second. (From Naches drive US 410 west about 12 miles to this road.) At 1.4 miles from the highway turn left on road No. 150 and stay on it, dodging numerous sideroads, 11.6 miles to a jeep track signed "Trail No. 981," elevation 3200 feet.

Walk the jeep road down to a creek crossing, which may be dry, contour to a Y, and take the uphill branch, left. At the next Y go right, climbing very steeply and dropping even more steeply to a crossing of Three Stream. Steeply up again, down again. At 1¾ miles the way comes to Rattlesnake Creek, where camping would be bliss were it not for the jockeys on two, three, four, and six wheels.

A last mile of jeep road leads to the wilderness boundary (which *must* be extended down the valley) and the start of true, quiet trail. But then, shortly beyond, at 3 miles, is that fearsome first ford, knee-deep even in

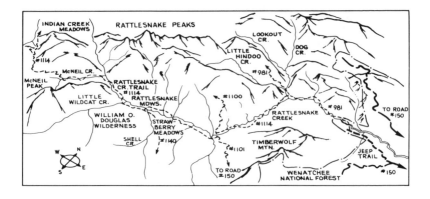

Rattlesnake Creek

low water. By late August or so, however, the wading is stimulating yet not perilous. As for the rest of the fords, none quite so menacing, some can be avoided, some years, by following game traces along the stream bed.

At 4½ miles is a junction. The right fork is an arduous climb to Justice Douglas' favorite, Hindoo Valley, a trip on its own. To complete the Rattlesnake, however, go left on trail No. 1114, up and down steeply. At 7½ miles pass trail No. 1101, an alternate route from road No. 150. At 9½ miles cross the Rattlesnake the fourteenth and last time near Strawberry Meadows. At 10 miles ramble into Rattlesnake Meadows, 3900 feet.

The trail continues 7 more miles to Indian Creek Meadows, well worth doing. If that is the destination, however, there are quicker routes (Hike 27).

Old road: 150
New road: 150

25 CARLTON CREEK— FISH LAKE

Round trip 7½ miles
Hiking time 5 hours
High point 4150 feet
Elevation gain 1100 feet

Hikable mid-July through
  October
One day or backpack
USGS White Pass and Bumping
  Lake

A rough trail ascends old-growth forest to the Cascade Crest, in country that is late-winter range for the elk that browse on brush in nearby clearcuts, then retire to rest in deep forest where the snow depth is less. Though there is some horse damage, it's mainly the elk that churn the trail to mud, exposing tree roots that grab for the hiker's ankles, making for slow and careworn going. The best walking is in late summer and fall when the mud has dried; the roots are still there.

Drive Highway 410 to Cayuse Pass and turn south on Highway 123 to .2 mile beyond the Rainier National Park entrance (from this direction, the exit) and turn uphill on road No. 44. (From US 12 drive Highway 123 north 2.2 miles.) In 5.8 miles find Carlton Creek trail No. 22, elevation 3100 feet.

Start on a jeep road leading to a crossing of Carlton Creek. If the water is too high for boulder hopping, go upstream a hundred feet to a good log. Proceed beyond on abandoned logging road, skirt a clearcut (note how the brush has been elk nibbled), and enter virgin forest.

In about ½ mile cross a creek in sound but not sight of a spectacular waterfall. (To see it, walk upstream.) The next mile is through old-growth hemlock and fir, a company of ancient giants protected within the William O. Douglas Wilderness.

At about 2¾ miles is a campsite in the woods. At 3½ miles reach 4150-foot Carlton Pass and descend to Fish Lake and a junction with the Pacific Crest Trail, 4114 feet, 3¾ miles from the road.

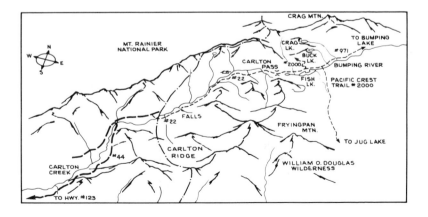

Fish Lake

Fish Lake is shallow and swampy and is not the scenic climax of this hike. The forests are. For higher excitement, follow the Crest Trail north, climbing into pretty flowers and broad views.

Old road: 1500
New road: 44

Small pond near Frying Pan Lake

COWLITZ RIVER
William O. Douglas Wilderness

26 FRYINGPAN LOOP

Round trip 14½ miles
Allow 2 days
High point 5200 feet
Elevation gain 2000 feet

Hikable mid-July through
   October
One day or backpack
USGS White Pass

The low-top forests of subalpine trees with intimate green meadows interspersed, the wildflowers and lakes and lakes, the birds and the bees and the chipmunks, are enough to fill a day. Overnight is better. The counterclockwise loop is recommended to avoid hauling a pack steeply to Jug Lake. Day hikers can shorten the loop to 9½ miles.

Candidly, the trip has four problems, one natural, three human-caused. **Mosquitoes:** Walk fast, carry repellent, don't go until the frosts of September. **Signs:** Some junctions have no signs, and at some that do, the signs give only numbers. **Maps:** Some Forest Service maps do not show all the trails, and many trails are missing from the USGS maps, so a hiker must carry a weighty mass of paper. **Horses:** The cavalry rides this region in numbers approaching the squadrons of Phil Sheridan, Jeb Stuart, and the Cossacks, and where trails are wet, horses churn the soil to mud and a hiker may simply sink out of sight in black muck and nevermore be seen.

Drive US 12 east 1.3 miles from Highway 123 and turn left on road No. 45. In .3 mile turn left on road No. 4570. At 4.5 miles from the highway turn right on Soda Springs Campground road to its end in 5 miles, elevation 3200 feet.

At the far end of the campground set out on Cowlitz trail No. 44. In 2 miles intersect Jug Lake trail and continue on No. 44, now signed "Penoyer Lake," to a four-way junction at 4 miles of trails Nos. 41, 44, and 45. For the shorter day hike, saving about 3 miles, take No. 45. Mosquito-undaunted backpackers proceed on No. 44 to Penoyer Lake, 5000 feet, 4¾ miles, and splendid camping.

The second day continue 1¾ miles on No. 44 to the Pacific Crest Trail, 5191 feet, 6½ miles from the road. Turn north on the Crest Trail, gently up and down, passing numerous lakes and ponds and marshes, 2 miles to a four-way stop. To the right, No. 980 goes a near-level 1½ miles to Twin Sisters Lakes (Hike 23). To the left, No. 46 goes directly to Fryingpan Lake. Instead, continue on the Crest Trail 1 more mile and turn left on Jug Lake trail No. 43.

In ½ mile pass Fryingpan Lake amid large meadows, continue on by long and narrow little Snow Lake and lose 400 feet, passing No. 41, to a ¼-mile spur path to ever-popular Jug Lake, 4416 feet, 2 miles from the Crest Trail.

Beyond the spur No. 43 levels briefly and plunges 400 feet to the Cowlitz trail, which returns the looper 2 miles to the start, completing the 14½ miles.

Old road: 145   1400
New road: 45   4570

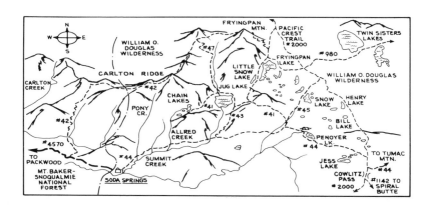

27 INDIAN CREEK– BLANKENSHIP LAKES

**Round trip to Blankenship Lakes
12 miles
Hiking time 6 hours
High point 5200 feet
Elevation gain 2000 feet in, 200
feet out**

**Hikable mid-July through
October
One day or backpack
USGS White Pass**

Pocket-size meadows, vast grasslands, and beautiful mountain lakes make this country unique in the Cascades. The map calls the area "Mosquito Valley," and rightly so. Though the meadows are magnificent when bright green, the bugs are then numbered by the billions; the hike is much more enjoyable in late summer and fall.

Besides a USGS map, a party *must carry* a Forest Service map, because the local signing system gives only trail numbers instead of place names, guaranteed to confuse and lose anyone who forgets his map.

Drive US 12 east from White Pass 8.3 miles. A few hundred feet before Indian Creek Campground, turn left on road No. 1308, signed "Bootjack Summer Homes." Drive .8 mile to a junction and keep left, still on road No. 1308; at 3 miles from the highway is the parking lot by the trailhead sign, Indian Creek trail, No. 1105, elevation 3400 feet.

The first 2 miles of trail are an old mining road, now closed because ¼ mile from the start it enters the William O. Douglas Wilderness. Just before the end of the road, find the start of true trail, which drops steeply 200 feet into a canyon, crosses Indian Creek, and climbs very steeply out of the canyon. At about 2½ miles listen for a waterfall to the right; the canyon edge and a view of the lovely falls are just a few feet off the path, though one may have to try a couple of spots before finding the only really good vantage point.

The trail crosses Indian Creek again at about 3 miles, recrosses at 4

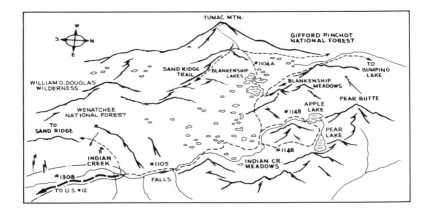

Blankenship Lake and Tumac Mountain

miles, and at 4½ miles enters the large (⅓-mile-long) Indian Creek Meadows. Stay on trail No. 1105, passing trail No. 1148 to Pear and Apple Lakes. The tread is faint as it traverses the meadow and heads west, but becomes distinct again beyond the grass. At 5 miles pass trail No. 1148 to Apple Lake, and at just under 6 miles take a short sidetrail to the first of the three Blankenship Lakes, 5200 feet, a fair spot for a basecamp.

The first thing to do is explore the other two lakes, a stone's throw from each other. Next comes the ascent of 6340-foot Tumac Mountain, a small volcano rising over the lakes and offering superb views; two trails lead to the top from other sides (Hike 23) but a path really isn't needed. Follow trail No. 1104A between the lakes, climbing to its junction with the Sand Ridge trail. Continue uphill, off-trail, to the summit, avoiding soft cinder slopes.

Another ½ mile along trail No. 1105 are Blankenship Meadows—many little clearings and one huge expanse. As is true of many other meadows in this portion of the Cascades, young trees are invading the grass. There are strangely few flowers in the meadows, but beargrass and lupine grow in the woods, and bog orchids and elephantheads in wet places. (Blankenship Meadows can also be reached by a 4-mile hike from road No. 162, near Bumping Lake.)

A 2-mile sidetrip to Pear and Apple Lakes is a must. This can be done as a one-way walk, going first to shallow Apple Lake on trail No. 1148, then continuing on the same trail to deep Pear Lake, and returning to the main route on trail No. 1148.

Good camps at Indian Creek Meadows, Blankenship Lakes, and Pear Lake. To preserve the vegetation, camp at least 100 feet from lakeshores.

Old road: 1410
New road: 1308

28   SPIRAL BUTTE

Round trip from Dog Lake 17 miles	**Round trip via Sand Ridge 13 miles**
Allow 2 days	**Hiking time 8 hours**
High point 5800 feet	**Elevation gain 2500 feet**
Elevation gain 1800 feet	**Hikable early July through September**
Hikable mid-July through September	**One day**
USGS White Pass	

North of White Pass the Cascade Crest is a broad lava plateau, dominated by two very young (postglacial) and comparatively small volcanoes, Tumac Mountain (Hike 23) at the north end, and, at the south, Spiral Butte (originally Big Peak), rising 1600 feet directly above Dog Lake. Summit views are across the plateau to Tumac, down to the White Pass ski area, and out to Rainier and the Goat Rocks.

There are two approaches. The round trip from Dog Lake is 17 miles with an elevation gain, counting ups and downs, of 1800 feet, rather much for one day. The round trip via Sand Ridge is 4 miles shorter, possible in a day, though the elevation gain, with ups and downs, is 2500 feet; this route is snow free several weeks earlier than the other.

From Dog Lake: Drive US 12 east 2 miles from White Pass to Dog Lake Campground, elevation 4300 feet.

Take Cramer Lake trail No. 1106, at 3 miles passing Cramer Lake. At 3½ miles turn right on a short connecting trail (no number shown), then right again on Shellrock Lake trail No. 1142, passing the lake. At 6½ up-and-down miles from Dog Lake reach Spiral Butte (sometimes signed "Big Peak") trail No. 1108, 4800 feet.

The initial scant ½ mile gains 400 feet without a switchback (steep). The final 1½ miles along a wooded ridge crest gain their 600 feet more

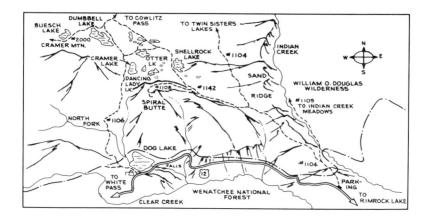

Dog Lake from Spiral Butte

reasonably. Just below the summit is an old burn with views of Rainier, Tumac, Aix, and Bismark. From the 5800-foot top gaze straight down to toy boats on Dog Lake and out over White Pass to the Goat Rocks.

Via Sand Ridge: Drive US 12 east 6.4 miles from White Pass to Sand Ridge trail No. 1104, elevation 3400 feet. Probably used by Indians, and certainly by stockmen driving cattle west from Tieton country over Cowlitz Pass, the trail is mentioned by William O. Douglas in *Of Men and Mountains*.

Trail No. 1104 climbs steadily 2 miles, mainly on a ridge crest with more ups than downs. At 3 miles go left on Shellrock Lake trail No. 1142, and in another 1½ miles reach the Spiral Butte trail and proceed to the summit.

29 SAND AND DUMBBELL LAKES

Round trip to Sand Lake 6 miles
Hiking time 4 hours
High point 5295 feet
Elevation gain 900 feet
Hikable mid-July through
November
One day
USGS White Pass

Round trip to Dumbbell Lake 13
miles
Hiking time 7 hours
High point 5600 feet
Elevation gain 1200 feet in, 500
feet out
Hikable mid-July through
November
One day or backpack

If you like alpine lakes, this is certainly the trail—there are dozens of them, large and small. If you like tall, picturesque alpine trees, this is the trail—there are thousands of lovely specimens. And if you like fall hiking through the bright red leaves of huckleberry bushes, this is the trail—there are miles of color. The hike along a delightful section of the Pacific Crest Trail can be done as a day trip to Sand Lake or an overnight to Dumbbell Lake.

Fog blowing over Sand Lake

Drive US 12 east from White Pass .7 mile, turn left into White Pass Campground, and continue about .25 mile to the trailhead near Leech Lake, elevation 4412 feet. This is Pacific Crest Trail No. 2000. A new and very confusing system of signing gives trail numbers rather than destinations. There is no problem so long as a party stays on the Crest Trail, but any deviation requires a Forest Service map to decipher the signs.

The trail starts in forest, climbing 800 feet in 2½ miles to Deer Lake, 5206 feet, still in woods. At 3 miles is Sand Lake, 5295 feet, with numerous arms surrounded by meadows and alpine trees. Though the water is very clear, the shallow lake seems to have neither inlet nor outlet. Sand Lake is an excellent turnaround for day hikers. (Many a person who long had wondered why the lakes hereabouts are so sandy understood after St. Helens lost its head.)

Now the trail wanders past numerous small lakes, climbing to 5600 feet at 4 miles. Several places offer glimpses southward of Mt. Adams and the Goat Rocks; Spiral Butte can be seen through the trees to the east.

At about 5 miles the trail switches from the east side of the crest to the west and descends in forest, losing 500 feet in ¾ mile. Now and then Mt. Rainier can be partly viewed through trees; for a better look walk off the trail 100 feet onto a low, rocky knoll located on the left side of the path soon after passing two small ponds.

At 6 miles the way skirts Buesch Lake, 5081 feet, and reaches a junction with Cramer Lake trail No. 1106. Follow this a short ¼ mile to Dumbbell Lake, 5091 feet. Much of the lake is shallow; the rocky shoreline is very interesting. To appreciate its unusual shape, beat through a patch of brush and scramble to the bald summit of 5992-foot Cramer Mountain—and views much broader than merely the lake.

For an alternate return, follow Cramer Lake trail No. 1106 down to within ½ mile of Dog Lake, turn west on Dark Meadow trail No. 1107, and finish with a last mile on the Crest Trail. The distance is about the same but most of the way is in forest.

To preserve vegetation, camp at least 100 feet from lakeshores.

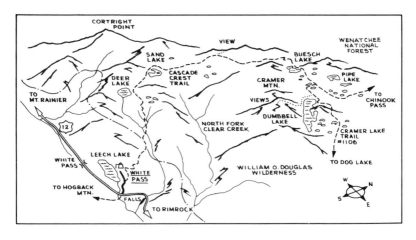

Mount Beljica

NISQUALLY RIVER
Glacier View Wilderness

 MOUNT BELJICA AND GOAT LAKE

Round trip 8 miles
Hiking time 5 hours
High point 5478 feet
Elevation gain 1300 feet in, 600
feet out

Hikable mid-July through
October
One day or backpack
USGS Mt. Wow

On a summer day when the hikers on trails of Mt. Rainier National Park outnumber the flowers, dodge away to Glacier View Wilderness, with meadows and lakes to match any in the park and an unsurpassed view of The Mountain, featuring the mighty Tahoma Glacier tumbling from the summit icecap virtually to the forests.

Drive Highway 706 (the way to the park's Nisqually entrance) 3 miles past Ashford and turn left on Copper Creek road No. 59. At a junction in 3.4 miles keep left, at 5 miles turn right on road No. 5920, and in 6.5 miles reach Lake Christine trailhead, elevation 4400 feet.

Trail No. 249 sternly ascends a ridge, then eases its grade to traverse a very steep sidehill to Lake Christine, 1 mile, 4802 feet. Continue past the small, forest-ringed lake and climb a bit to an unmarked and easy-to-miss junction. Turn left on the unmaintained trail ½ mile to the summit of 5478-foot Mt. Beljica. Anonymous until climbed in 1897 by members of the Mesler and LaWall families, the peak's name consists of the first letters of Burgon, Elizabeth, Lucy, Jessie, Isabel, Clara, and Alex.

Fill your eyes, exhaust your camera film, return to the trail, and—if the trip is overnight—descend 600 feet more, passing a shortcut trail to road No. 59, and at 3½ miles from the car find campsites at Goat Lake, 4342 feet.

The trail continues, and so can the trip, to Gobblers Knob in Mt. Rainier National Park.

Old road:	159	159B
New road:	59	5920

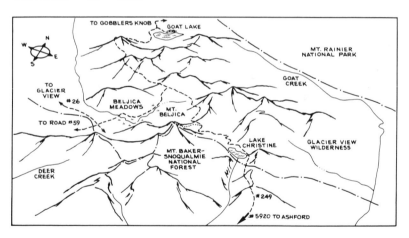

31 GLACIER VIEW AND LAKE WEST

Round trip 6 miles
Hiking time 3 hours
High point 5450 feet
Elevation gain 1100 feet

Hikable July through October
One day
USGS Mt. Wow

Mt. Rainier—The Mountain—perhaps must be climbed to the crater, or at least explored in the zone of glacier snouts and moraines and lava cleavers, to be fully *felt*. But it is best *seen* at something of a distance, where the neck doesn't get a crick from bending back. An old fire lookout site in a new wilderness area provides a connoisseur's perspective, superior to any in the Paradise vicinity—and on a fine summer day having a hundredth or a thousandth of the human population. For added entertainment there are sidetrails to a pair of little lakes and a lovely little meadow.

Drive Copper Creek road No. 59 (Hike 30) 7.6 miles to a ridge crossing with an outstanding view of Rainier. Continue on, going straight ahead at 8.4 miles and at 9.1 miles reaching the trailhead, elevation 4400 feet.

A short trail climbs to intersect trail No. 267, built in the 1930s to help the Forest Service protect the forests from fire, 15 miles of it obliterated by the roads with which the Forest Service cut the forests. No. 267 parallels the road a bit, often a stone's throw from clearcuts, and enters the Glacier View Wilderness at the start of a ridge extending northward.

Hardly has the hike got going when a junction presents alternatives. Save the right fork for the return, a ¼-mile level stroll to Beljica Meadows, 4400 feet, a cozy marsh-meadow at the foot of Mt. Beljica (Hike 30); this trail continues to Goat Lake.

Go left, signed "Glacier View," along the ridge, swinging around the forested slopes of one of its summits and around the meadowy-rocky-woodsy slopes of another, to a saddle 2½ miles from the road. Here the trail splits. The right fork drops 600 feet in a scant mile to tiny Lake West, Lake Helen beyond, the pair worth an hour or two for collectors of lakes and fish.

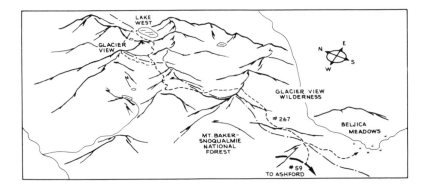

Mount Rainier from site of Glacier View Lookout (Vicky Spring photo)

The left fork proceeds ⅓ mile along a splinter of andesite to the 5450-foot summit, once the site of Glacier View Lookout. You'll understand *why* a fire lookout was here. To the west then, and the north and south, the view commanded hundreds of square miles of virgin forest—and now, hundreds of square miles of second-growth and raw, new clearcuts.

To the east . . . the first hour you will simply gaze. Then you'll want to get out your map and methodically identify the glaciers, notably the monster ice streams of the Puyallup and Tahoma, and Sunset Ridge and Tokaloo Rock and Success Cleaver, and Klapatche Park and St. Andrews Park. By then maybe you'll be ready to visit the flowers in Beljica Meadows.

Old road: 159
New road: 59

32 TATOOSH RIDGE

Round trip to viewpoint 6 miles
Hiking time 4 hours
High point 5400 feet
Elevation gain 2600 feet

Hikable July through September
One day; possible camping at lake
USGS Packwood

A long ridge with flower meadows and a beautiful lake lies under the dominance of Mt. Rainier, giving views not only of The Mountain but the backside of the Tatoosh Range, whose peaks are familiar as seen from Paradise but except for Pinnacle are difficult to recognize from here. On the highest point is the site of the Tatoosh Lookout made famous in the 1940s by Martha Hardy's bestselling book, *Tatoosh,* the story of her years as a fire lookout. (The book was reprinted in the 1980s.) "Belonging" to Rainier National Park but outside the boundaries, the ridge long has been proposed for addition to the park; that has not yet happened, but the wildland vista Martha Hardy celebrated *has* been largely protected by the Tatoosh Wilderness.

The trail covers the full length of the ridge, starting in the south near Packwood and ending in the north on a logging road near the park boundary. If transportation can be arranged, the entire distance can be done on one trip. It is described here from a north-end start because that way has 1000 feet less elevation gain.

From Packwood Ranger Station at the north end of Packwood, drive west on Skate Creek road No. 52. In .5 mile cross the Cowlitz River. (To start on the south end of the ridge, cross the bridge and turn right on Cannon road which eventually becomes road No. 5290. Follow this up-river 9 miles and turn right on road No. 5292 for 1.2 miles to the trailhead.) For the north end continue on Skate Creek road 4 miles from the ranger station (sign says 3), turn north on road No. 5270, drive 5.8 miles to a junction, and there continue ahead on No. 5272 for 1.5 miles to the trailhead, elevation 2800 feet.

Trail No. 161 sets off at a steep grade, gaining about 1800 feet in 2 miles, climbing from Douglas fir forest to Alaska cedar and mountain hemlock. At about 2½ miles begin steep alpine meadows, covered in sea-

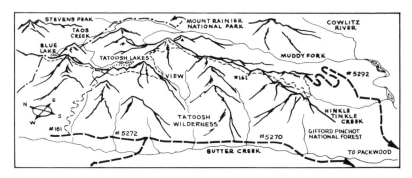

Tatoosh Lake and Mount Rainier

son with colorful blossoms. The trail makes three short switchbacks up a small stream, the only water on the main route—and maybe none here late in summer. Shortly beyond is an unmarked junction. Proceed straight ahead but keep the junction in mind for later reference. Tread may be lost in lush greenery and soft pumice; just keep going and eventually gain a ridge shoulder, 5400 feet, and a spectacular view of Mt. Adams, St. Helens, and the Cowlitz valley. To the north Mt. Rainier looks down like a benevolent old lady, very fat.

After soaking up views, there are things to do, more to see. For one, continue on the trail another 1½ miles and find the mile-long spur trail climbing to the Tatoosh Lookout site at 6310 feet, highest point on the ridge outside the park. Second, retrace steps to that unmarked junction and follow an old trail to the park boundary. Or, if experienced in wildland navigation and possessed of the USGS map, try to find Tatoosh Lakes, a small one and a large one, on the east side of Tatoosh Ridge. From the aforementioned junction an unmarked trail of sorts switchbacks up, crosses a 5500-foot saddle, and drops to the lakes near the outlet. But the trail can be hard to follow and cliffs make cross-country travel tricky.

Skate Creek road—Old:		152		
	New:	52		
Old road:	1412	1412A	1411	1411B
New road:	5290	5292	5270	5272

33 HIGH ROCK

Round trip 3 miles
Hiking time 2 hours
High point 5685 feet
Elevation gain 1400 feet

Hikable June through October
One day
USGS Randle

A short but steady climb to a lookout with a breathtaking view of Mt. Rainier. The cabin sits on a point of rock like the prow of a ship. Once this was a challenging hike, but now, in common with most Forest Service trails south of Rainier, is only an afternoon walk—or better, a morning walk, when the lighting is more striking. A good trip for small children, but hold their hands tight on the last bit to the summit.

Drive Highway 706 east from Ashford 3.8 miles and turn right on Kernahan Road, signed "Big Creek Campground—Packwood." From this junction drive about 1 mile to a crossing of the Nisqually River on a steel bridge. At 1.5 miles is a junction. The easiest way to the trailhead is to go right on road No. 85 to Towhead Gap, elevation 4301 feet. However, if sidetrips to Cora, Bertha May, or Granite Lakes are contemplated, go left on road No. 52, signed "Packwood." At 4.3 miles turn right on road No. 8400, cross Big Creek and start climbing. At 11.3 miles keep right on road No. 8400 and at 14 miles reach Towhead Gap.

Trail No. 266 starts on the north side of the gap, ascends a few hundred feet in a logged-off patch, and enters forest. The first mile is mostly through trees, gradually thinning. The final ½ mile to the lookout is fairly open, with views to Mt. Adams and Mt. St. Helens.

Climaxing all is the eye-popping panorama of Mt. Rainier. Nowhere in the national park does one get this magnificent sweep from Columbia Crest down to the Nisqually entrance. Observe the outwash from the

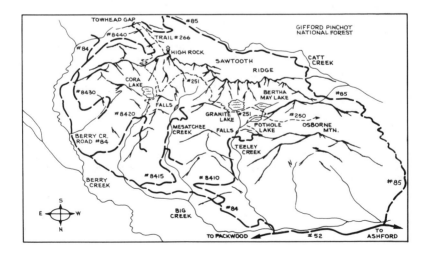

High Rock Lookout

catastrophic 1947 flood of Kautz Creek. Note hanging ice on the Kautz Glacier. Pick out peaks of the Tatoosh Range and Mt. Wow. See the green gardens of Indian Henry's Hunting Ground. When your eye shifts from The Mountain to your feet, hang on! Cora Lake is 1500 feet below, almost in spitting distance.

In midday Rainier is a big, flat curtain of white. The best views are when the sun slants over the face of the mountain, the contrast of bright light and dark shadows delineating every ridge and valley, even the trees in the parklands and crevasses on glaciers. Therefore plan to be at the lookout before 10 in the morning or after 4 in the afternoon.

To while away the heat and flat light of midday, before or after the summit climb, visit lovely Cora Lake, reached by a ½-mile trail from road No. 8420, a spur from Big Creek road No. 84, or Bertha May and Granite Lakes, reached by a 1-mile trail from Teeley Creek road No. 8410. A very nice 3-mile trail runs along under Sawtooth Ridge, connecting the lakes, but logging roads are so close, and trail bikes so numerous, that the lakes are mobbed by noisemakers. A dirty shame. The Forest Service could have made it otherwise.

Old road:	152	149	158
New road:	52	84	85

34
TRAILS END
(PURCELL MOUNTAIN)

**Round trip via Purcell Mountain
  trail 16 miles**
Allow 2 days
High point 5442 feet
Elevation gain 4500 feet
Hikable July through November
USGS Randle

**Round trip via lookout trail 7
  miles**
**Hiking time 6 hours (unless
  maintained)**
Elevation gain 2600 feet
**Hikable mid-June through
  November**
One day or backpack

A basin of subalpine trees and a large flower-covered meadow, topped by 5442-foot Purcell Mountain, site of Trails End Lookout. Nothing remains except melted glass, nails, a few bits of rusty iron, a heliport, and a panorama of the South Cascades.

A few years back the Forest Service built a logging road to the 3500-foot level. Hikers complained but it did no good—or did it? Since then a switch has been made from roading to helicopter logging, small solace for the trees but it does preserve the trail system.

There are two approaches: the long Purcell Mountain trail which traverses the entire length of the mountain, and the lookout trail climbing directly to the summit. Snow remains on the longer route until early July, but the direct route can be hiked in mid-June with only a few snow patches up high.

Whalehead Ridge from Purcell Mountain trail

Drive US 12 east from Randle toward Packwood. For the Purcell Mountain trail, at 5.6 miles, where the highway skirts the mountain, find the trailhead, elevation 920 feet. Park on the south side of the highway 75 yards east of the trailhead. The way crosses private land; if the owners say *No Trespassing,* take the other trail, described below.

The trail starts from the valley bottom and switchbacks upward in a 170-year-old stand of timber, gaining 2500 feet in 3 miles. The trees provide shade but the slope faces south and has no dependable water, so carry loaded canteens. At 3 miles the trail passes "The Gate"—a local landmark, though the gate has been gone a long time—and makes a big switchback. The way is still up, but the views improve. At 3½ miles is a junction with a path to springs and open meadows, 4400 feet, under Cockscomb Mountain. Now the trail levels off, still in timber, ascending slightly under 5065-foot Prairie Mountain. At approximately 5 miles is Little Paradise, 4800 feet, a small meadow surrounded by tall trees; water and camps can be found a bit below the meadow.

What to do now? One choice is to wander the short distance up Prairie Mountain; all but the summit and steep south side are wooded. The other choice is to continue 3 more miles to the top of Purcell Mountain and the panoramas.

For the lookout trail, continue .3 mile past the Purcell Mountain trailhead, turn left on an unmarked paved road (the old highway), and in 1 mile turn left on road No. 63. In a mile look over the side of the Davis Creek bridge into a spectacular canyon. At 4.5 miles from the paved road (11.5 miles from Randle) bear left onto road No. 6310 and in .5 mile cross Davis Creek and a short distance farther find the trailhead, elevation 2800 feet.

The route follows an abandoned road. In about ⅓ mile the trail doubles back to the right off the road and zigzags upward through a clearing, then forest. At 2½ miles the way reaches meadows and continues upward. At 3 miles, 5000 feet, just before the junction with the Purcell Mountain trail, is a possible camp. A final ½ mile climbs to the summit.

Davis Creek road—Old:	1303	Spur road—Old:	1303C
New:	63	New:	6310

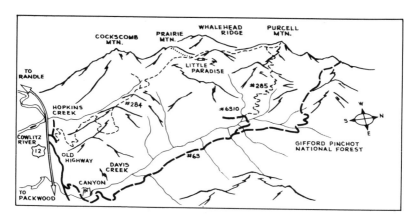

35 KLICKITAT TRAIL

One-way trip 17 miles	Hikable mid-July through
Allow 2–3 days	October
High point 5400 feet	USGS Tower Rock, Blue Lake,
Elevation gain 4000 feet	Hamilton Buttes

Tradition says this is part of the trail followed by the Klickitats on trading excursions from their homes east of the Cascades, climbing from the Klickitat River to Cispus Pass (Hike 44), then descending to Puget Sound country.

But the European has come, and though the trail is lonesome, seldom is it beyond sight or sound of logging. The way is paralleled by logging roads, cut once by a road (near Jackpot Lake), and hacked by several clearcuts. Only time will tell whether the Forest Service will adopt true multiple use of the land and preserve this rewarding trail.

To reach the west terminus of the trail, turn south in Randle, cross the Cowlitz River, and in 1 mile keep left on road No. 23. At 6 miles turn left on road No. 55 and in 15 miles (from Randle) turn left on road No. (5508)024 and in 1 mile find the trailhead, elevation 4000 feet.

To reach the east terminus, drive US 12 south from Packwood 2.5 miles, turn east on Johnson Creek road No. 21, and in 16.5 miles (from Packwood), just beyond Hugo Lake, turn right on road No. 22 and in 3.5 miles reach the trailhead, elevation approximately 4000 feet.

Signs at both ends call it "Klickitat Trail No. 7." By consulting a current Forest Service map, hikers can intersect the trail by climbing clearcuts from logging roads but in doing so would lose a lot of the fun. The mileages and elevations given here are estimates; there are some mile markers along the route, but no indication where the counting starts.

From the west terminus, the trail climbs 500 feet, follows the ridge top, and in a bit more than a mile drops steeply to a clearcut. Once beyond

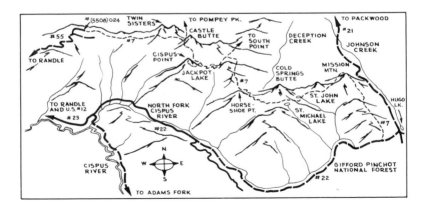

Mount Rainier from Cispus Point

this, the way passes under 5805-foot Twin Sisters and at about 4 miles, 5200 feet, comes to a junction with the Pompey Peak trail.

The next 1½ miles are a glorious combination of alpine meadows and forest groves. Castle Butte towers above. At Cispus Point, 5½ miles, are campsites. An absolute must is the ½-mile sidetrip to the site of the old lookout and wide views of Rainier, Adams, St. Helens, Hood, and ridge upon forested ridge.

Now the trail descends into timber, dropping almost 1000 feet to Jackpot Lake, 6 miles, 4500 feet, and another clearcut. A traverse near the top of a 5500-foot butte offers more views. At 8 miles the route drops into headwaters of Deception Creek, crosses clearcuts, and at 9 miles contours under Horsehoe Point and gradually ascends to a saddle below 5733-foot Cold Springs Butte. Along here the tread is particularly faint. The short sidetrip to the summit of the butte is well worth the effort.

The path drops through forest to campsites at St. Michael Lake, 10½ miles, 4700 feet, contours past tiny St. John Lake, climbs nearly over the top of 5683-foot Mission Mountain, and goes downward in trees, passing a junction with the Elk Peak trail at 15¾ miles and at 17 miles reaching the east terminus on road No. 22.

Old road:	121	123	1302	1111	1216B
New road:	55	23	21	22	(5508)024

36   BLUE LAKE

**Round trip via first Blue Lake
trail 6 miles**
Hiking time 4 hours
High point 4000 feet
Elevation gain 2100 feet
**Hikable mid-June through
November**
One day or backpack
USGS none

**Round trip via Bishop Ridge trail
21 miles**
Allow 2–3 days
High point 5200 feet
**Elevation gain 3600 feet in, 1200
feet out**
**Hikable mid-June through
November**

A captivating lake nestled in a basin, surrounded by forest. There are three routes to the truly blue waters: a first Blue Lake trail, 3 miles, in timber the whole way and crowded by people and machines; Bishop Ridge, a tough 10 miles with glorious views; and a second Blue Lake trail, 9 miles, all in timber. Any two can be combined to make a loop trip; if the combination includes the view route, save that for the way home and avoid a grueling climb out of the valley.

Turn south in Randle, cross the Cowlitz River, and drive 1 mile. Turn left on road No. 23 for 13 miles (from Randle) and find the Bishop Ridge trail on the left side of the road. In 17 miles find the first Blue Lake trail

Blue Lake from Bishop Ridge

on the left side of the road. At 19 miles keep left on road No. 21 and at 25 miles, just past the Adams Fork Campground sign, find the second Blue Lake trail (via Mouse Lake), also on the left.

The shortest way is via the first Blue Lake trail, No. 271, which starts from an elevation of 1900 feet and ascends steadily through tall fir trees, crossing Blue Lake Creek in sound of a waterfall and at 3 miles reaching the 4000-foot lake near the outlet. The best camps are here, but if crowded, poorer sites can be found at the upper end.

Bishop Ridge trail No. 272 starts at 1600 feet and switchbacks relentlessly upward 4 miles to the ridge top, about 4600 feet. The path offers considerable shade but can be hot, so carry water—there is none after the first ¾ mile. Going often up and occasionally down, the trail follows the crest, which at 5 miles becomes very narrow. Between 5½ and 6 miles is the location of a planned timber sale; the Forest Service intends to obliterate the logging road after the cutting is finished, in order not to interrupt the hiking route.

The trail stays on the ridge top as it gradually rises to a 5200-foot saddle, 7 miles, between Blue Lake and Yozoo Creek. Views here are magnificent, and on clear days Blue Lake really lives up to its name. On the Yozoo Creek side is a small pond about ⅓ mile and 500 feet below the trail, a possible campsite. Soak up the scenery and then continue several hundred feet—Mt. St. Helens comes in sight, and sharp Tongue Mountain across the Cispus; farther downvalley are Tower Rock, farms, and Mayfield Reservoir.

From this spot the trail ducks under a 5683-foot high point on the ridge and drops to a junction with the second Blue Lake trail, No. 272, at 9½ miles, a short mile above the outlet.

The hike to Mouse Lake from Blue Lake, pass the Bishop Ridge trail, reaching Mouse Lake and campsites at 5 miles, 4500 feet. Descend 4 miles to the road, 2500 feet.

Old road: 123   1111   1302
New road: 23   22   21

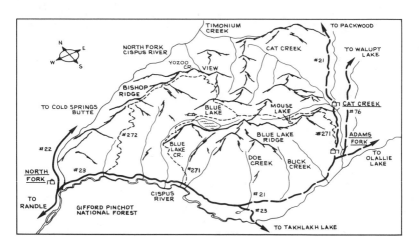

37 BEAR CREEK MOUNTAIN

Round trip 7½ miles
Hiking time 4 hours
High point 7335 feet
Elevation gain 1400 feet

Hikable mid-July through
  mid-October
One day or backpack
USGS White Pass, Forest Service
  Goat Rocks Wilderness

Amble through flowers and lawns and subalpine trees on slopes of a high ridge. Then shift down and ascend lava rocks of the old Goat Rocks Volcano to the summit of Bear Creek Mountain, 7335 feet, onetime site of a fire lookout with fabulous views up and down the Cascades.

When the St. Helens cannon went off it was pointed right at this spot; a month later the surveyor climbed from Conrad Meadows in gray ash that was inches thick atop the snow. Wind, water, and gravity are mingling the Event of 1980 with the many prior Events, but for years the hiker will find stretches of soft "beach."

The flowers are at their best in late July and early August, which is nice timing, because the road to the trailhead usually is snowbound until early July; if visiting before then, approach from Conrad Meadows (Hike 38).

Drive US 12 from White Pass and before reaching Rimrock Reservoir turn right on the paved road signed "Tieton Road" and "Clear Lake." Instructions in case some of the signs are missing, stolen by local funseekers: at 3.2 miles cross North Fork Tieton River, at 5.3 miles turn right on gravel road No. 1205, at 7.9 miles go straight, at 10 miles go left on No. (1205)757, at 10.9 miles go right (uphill) on No. 1204, at a junction at 12.2 miles go right (uphill) on nongravel and maybe rough and rude road. At 14.8 miles heave a sigh at the road-end and trailhead a few feet from the pond humorously called Section 3 "Lake," elevation approximately 6000 feet.

Trail No. 1130 is a dream, traversing wildflowers and Christmas trees and creeklets and many a lovely camp. At 2¼ miles is a junction with the

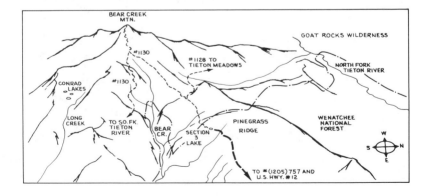

Goat Rocks from Bear Creek Mountain

trail from Conrad Meadows. From here the way winds up through gaudy rocks and cold-snowy nooks with a different array of flowers and still more possible camps and at 3¾ miles attains the summit. Look out to the great volcanoes of Rainier and Adams. Look around you, back down Pinegrass Ridge and to Devils Horns, Tieton, Old Snowy, and Gilbert and realize you are smack in the middle of a volcano that was worn out and broken down eons before St. Helens was so much as a puff of steam in a lowland swamp.

Old road:	1311	1311A	1311B	1314
New road:	1205	1205	(1205)757	1204

38 MEADE GLACIER– CONRAD GLACIER

**Round trip to Tieton–Conrad
divide 16 miles
Allow 3 days
High point 6000 feet
Elevation gain 2100 feet**

**Hikable July through September
USGS White Pass (part only),
Walupt Lake; Forest Service
Goat Rocks Wilderness**

Two glaciers on 8201-foot Gilbert Peak are sublimely scenic. So are black and gray and brown cliffs of Gilbert and Moon Mountain and yellow and red cliffs of Tieton Peak and brick-red spires of Devils Horns. But first the hiker must pass through miles of cow pies and horse apples, an experience that on a hot day requires a stiff upper lip. Morever, this area was directly in the mainline of 1980 ashing and for years the lower trails will be stirred to clouds of dust by passage of feet and hooves, and the camps will be sandy and the soup gritty.

Drive US 12 east from White Pass 19 miles, to just short of Hause Creek Campground, and turn right on South Fork Tieton road No. 12, heading back westward along Rimrock Lake. At 4.5 miles turn left on road No. 10 and stay with it at all junctions. At 18 miles the road is gated at the edge of private property. Park here, elevation 3900 feet.

South Fork Tieton trail No. 1120 passes the gate, fords Short Creek and Long Creek, at an obscure junction with Tenday trail goes right, and enters Conrad Meadows, the largest subalpine valley-bottom meadow in the Cascades. In the summer after The Blast, when ash kept out the cows, the vastness of lush, table-flat greenery glowed with approximately 17½ googols of flowers. Except after eruptions, however, this Paradise is closely cropped and reekingly flopped. Additionally, in the late 1970s some of the economically, ecologically, and esthetically least rational logging in the history of the world commenced in scraggly forests edging the meadows. The entirety of the valley ultimately must be added to the Goat Rocks Wilderness.

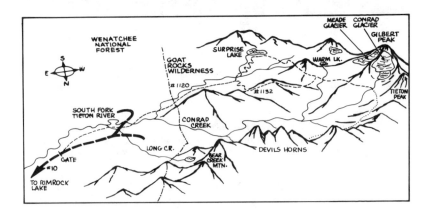

A shoulder of Gilbert Peak

At 1¼ miles trail No. 1120 (beware of misleading cow paths and cat roads) hits the logging road, turns left, and crosses the South Fork Tieton on remnants of a truck bridge; when this is finally gone, expect a ford that in early summer will be quite formidable. Where the road heads uphill (a private section was logged in the early 1970s by Boise Cascade) the trail goes off right. At 2 miles it fords the South Fork, here a mere creek. The way alternates between open forest and small meadows to enter Goat Rocks Wilderness at 2½ miles and at 4¼ miles, 4250 feet, reach a junction in a hellebore meadow. Campsites here.

Goat Rocks trail No. 1132 goes right, across the meadow, ascends steeply and roughly to the crest of the divide ridge between the South Fork Tieton and Conrad Creek, and proceeds gently to a 6000-foot saddle about 3 miles from the junction; here it drops off the ridge to headwaters of the South Fork.

From the junction, trail No. 1120 fords the South Fork and switchbacks steeply to Surprise Lake, 5300 feet, 6 miles, a fishy hole in the woods stomped and fouled by horses whose owners don't give a darn. Nicer camping is a bit beyond the lake, where the trail opens out in meadows on its ascent across the valley head to the 6000-foot saddle, attained at about 8 miles.

The saddle is the end of trail hiking, the start of off-trail roaming in all directions: to the Meade Glacier, to Warm Lake, to the Conrad Glacier, to Cold Lake.

Many fine and private camps are scattered about. However, the fragile meadows are so readily churned by hooves that the Forest Service *must* ban horses; it should build a corral at the 6000-foot saddle and tell all comers that to go beyond they must park and walk. To date, however, it has insisted that there is for horses, as for hikers, the possibility of "no-trace camping." It is to laugh!

Old road: 143   133
New road: 12   10

39 SHOE LAKE

**Round trip from trailhead east of
White Pass 14 miles
Hiking time 7 hours
High point 6600 feet
Elevation gain 2200 feet in, 500
feet out
Hikable mid-July through
October
One day
USGS White Pass**

**Round trip from top of White Pass
chairlift 8 miles
Hiking time 4 hours
Elevation gain 900 feet in, 600 feet
out**

Meadows and parklands along the Cascade Crest, grand views of the Goat Rocks and Mt. Adams, and a beautiful lake (absolutely fish free, which is a mercy) in a green basin. All this on an easy day from the road.

Drive US 12 east from White Pass .7 mile to the parking lot and trailhead (Pacific Crest Trail) opposite Leech Lake Campground, elevation 4400 feet.

(Alternately, for a shorter hike, park at White Pass ski area, 4400 feet, climb the ski hill 1½ miles, and take a short path that intersects the Pacific Crest Trail at a point 3 miles from the trailhead described above. For an even quicker trip, some hikers ride the chairlift to the top.)

From the formal trailhead east of White Pass, the way traverses and switchbacks open forest, touching a ski run at one point, and at 3 miles, 5900 feet, intersects the ridge crest and the path from the top of the chairlift.

Now the trail ascends into gardens and scattered alpine trees on the slopes of Hogback Mountain and swings onto the west side of the crest, with a great view of Mt. Rainier. Attaining a 6400-foot saddle, the route contours steep, broad shale slopes on the east side of 6789-foot Hogback (an easy scramble from the trail to the summit) above the basin contain-

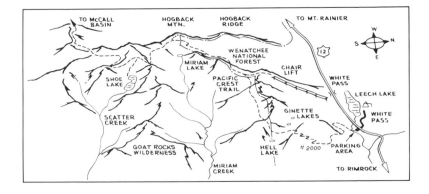

Shoe Lake

ing little Miriam Lake, and climbs to a 6600-foot saddle, 6½ miles, in a spur ridge—commanding views of the Goat Rocks and Mt. Adams. And below, the bright waters of Shoe Lake.

Drop ⅓ mile to the lake, 6200 feet, and fields of flowers. However, due to damage done by past overuse, camping has been banned in the entire basin so that meadows may have a chance to recover. Camping is permitted ½ mile beyond the lake, at Hidden Springs.

40 COWLITZ RIVER (CLEAR FORK)

Round trip to Camp Hagon 13 miles
Hiking time 8 hours
High point 3700 feet
Elevation gain 200 feet, plus many ups and downs

Hikable June through October
One day or backpack
USGS White Pass

Trees are the star of this show, miles of wilderness-preserved forest, and cold creeks rattling and babbling in green shadows, and a little meadow-marshy lake thrown in for the bog flowers and reeds and pol-

Clear Fork trail

liwogs. It's a scene for leisurely ambling and relaxed camping, listening to the thrushes and watching the ouzels.

Drive US 12 north from Packwood 4.4 miles and turn uphill 9 miles on road No. 46 to the end, elevation 3400 feet.

Clear Fork trail No. 61 whets the appetite with ¼ mile of jeep track through a clearcut, then enters virgin forest for the Goat Rocks Wilderness. The way undulates 1¾ miles to Lily Lake, yellow pond lilies blooming in season and hordes of mosquitoes swarming, climbs a bit and drops at 2½ miles to Skeeter Shelter and a junction with trail No. 76 and the Sand Lake trail No. 60. (This approach from the White Pass highway is slightly shorter than the one described here but involves dropping 600 feet to cross the Clear Fork and regaining 500 feet.)

The tread now deteriorates to ankle-tangling roots and the grade repeatedly rollercoasters. At 4 miles is a nice campsite beside the crossing of Coyote Creek. Chimney Creek is crossed at 5 miles. At 6½ miles, where the trail fords the Clear Fork, are fine campsites at Camp Hagon, 3600 feet.

Hikers wishing to continue can find safe logs spanning the river. An ascent of 1200 feet in 2½ miles leads to Tieton Pass and the Pacific Crest Trail.

Old road: 1406
New road: 46

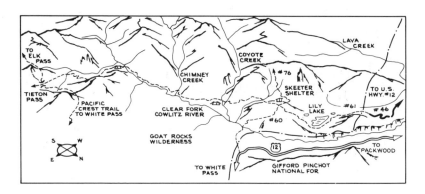

41   LOST LAKE

Round trip 12 miles
Hiking time 6 hours
High point 5165 feet
Elevation gain 2000 feet

Hikable July through October
One day or backpack
USGS Packwood

The little alpine lake amid meadows of lupine and lilies and paintbrush and beargrass, ringed by clumps of sturdy mountain trees, is abundant satisfaction. For more flowers—and bigger views—there is the 6359-foot site of an old lookout.

Four trails lead to Lost Lake: No. 76 from near White Pass; Bluff Lake trail No. 65 from road No. 4612; No. 78 from Packwood Lake (Hike 42); and Three Peaks trail No. 69, described here. All are steep, built in the 1930s for horses and long-legged young fire lookouts.

Drive US 12 north from Packwood Ranger Station 1.4 miles, turn right on Lost Creek Road 2.2 miles, turn right on road No. 1266, and at 7.5 miles from the ranger station find Three Peaks trailhead, elevation 3200 feet. (The last 1.5 miles may be too rough for some passenger cars.)

In the opening ½ mile the trail climbs steeply, skirts a clearcut, climbs again. Then the grade moderates to follow the crest of a narrow ridge, occasional windows in the forest giving views, including a glimpse of Packwood Lake. Pass a possible camp at 2½ miles. At 3¾ miles enter Goat Rocks Wilderness and at 5 miles join Packwood Lake trail No. 78 near Mosquito Lake, 4900 feet.

Go left, ascending gently through a small meadow with a huge view of the giant bulk of Johnson Peak. At 5½ miles pass Coyote trail No. 79 (to Elk Pass) and at 6 miles enter the flower carpet edging Lost Lake, 5165 feet. Nice camps.

If not yet full-up with pleasure, continue on the trail 1 more mile, climbing a steep cliff to a flowery knoll, 6359 feet, and panoramas of the Goat Rocks and other volcanoes.

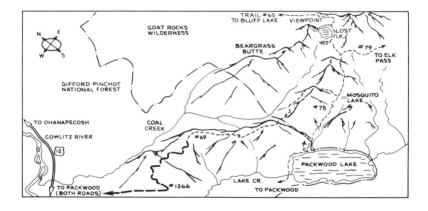

Johnson Peak from Lost Lake trail

Old road: 136
New road: 1266

Packwood Lake and Johnson Peak

COWLITZ RIVER
Goat Rocks Wilderness

PACKWOOD LAKE
AND SADDLE

Round trip to Packwood Lake 9
  miles
Hiking time 5 hours
High point 3100 feet
Elevation gain 400 feet, loss 300
  feet
Hikable June through November
One day or backpack
USGS Packwood

Round trip to Lost Lake 18¼ miles
Allow 2 days
High point 5165 feet
Elevation gain 2300 feet
Hikable July through October

A tree-ringed lake on the edge of the Goat Rocks Wilderness. From the outlet, look up to 7487-foot Johnson Peak. From the inlet, look back to Mt. Rainier. A wooded island punctuates the picturesque waters.

Unfortunately, man has left his mark on this scenic treasure—a potential disaster. Washington Public Power Supply System was allowed to dam the outlet to gain a small amount of "peaking" power and the Federal Power Commission mysteriously gave permission for the dam to be built 3 feet higher than specified in the agreement with the Forest Service. So far the power company has not been permitted to raise the lake above the natural level; if it ever is, the shore will be ruined.

Additionally, the trail was built so wide and flat and easy that every weekend the lake is overwhelmed by little children, old folk, motorbikers, horsemen, all jumbled together. Near the outlet are a small resort and a few campsites—terribly overcrowded. To avoid standing room only, visit the lake on a weekday; otherwise, pause amid the crowds to enjoy the view, then hike onward to Lost Lake.

Thanks to an easy trail, the lake is heavily used by hikers and horses. Though motorcycles are forbidden on the trail, they race up and down the adjoining pipeline road.

From Packwood, next to the Packwood Ranger Station, drive east on road No. 1260, in 6 miles coming to a steel tower and, nearby, a large parking lot and the trailhead, elevation 2700 feet.

Trail No. 78 goes gently through big trees with occasional views over the Cowlitz valley toward Rainier, passing several springs in the first half—but the second half is dry, so carry water. As the lake is neared, the snowy, craggy Goat Rocks can be seen at the valley head. With ups and downs grossing 400 feet but netting only 167 feet, at 4¼ miles the trail reaches Packwood Lake, 2867 feet.

For less jammed-up camping continue 4¾ miles to tiny Mosquito Lake, 4800 feet, or Lost Lake, 5165 feet, surrounded by alpine trees and flowery meadows (Hike 41).

For an extra-special treat, do a 12½-mile loop from Packwood Lake. Hike to Lost Lake and contour airy miles along 6700-foot Coyote Ridge on trail No. 79 to Packwood Saddle, 5520 feet. Return to Packwood Lake on Upper Lake trail No. 81. About half the distance is in steep meadows high above timberline. The way is little traveled, very odd considering the number of people at the lake and the superb scenery of the loop.

Old road: 1320
New road: 1260

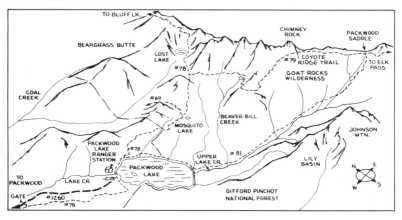

Packwood Lake and Mount Rainier from Lily Basin trail

COWLITZ RIVER
Goat Rocks Wilderness

 43

LILY BASIN—
HEART LAKE

Round trip to viewpoint 8 miles
Hiking time 5 hours
High point 5700 feet
Elevation gain 1300 feet
Hikable late July through
mid-October
One day
USGS Packwood

Round trip to Heart Lake 13 miles
Hiking time 8 hours
High point 6100 feet
Elevation gain 1700 feet in, 400
feet out
Backpack

Hike a forest ridge to a spectacular view of Packwood Lake and Mt. Rainier, then contour Lily Basin, a high cirque under Johnson Peak, and continue to Heart Lake and views of Mt. Adams. Logging roads to 4500 feet have ripped up the wildland and taken most of the work out of visiting this once-remote corner of the Goat Rocks.

Drive US 12 from Packwood Ranger Station west toward Randle 1.6 miles, passing the Packwood Lumber Company, and approximately opposite a small power substation turn left on road No. 48. Follow it 9 miles and turn left and stay on No. 48 another 1.2 miles to the trailhead, on the right side of the road. Park on a wide shoulder just beyond, elevation about 4400 feet.

The trail is signed "Lily Basin Trail No. 86." Climbing through timber to an old burn, at ½ mile the way enters Goat Rocks Wilderness and at 1½ miles reaches the crest of a wooded ridge, 4900 feet. The path follows ups and downs of the crest, more ups than downs, occasionally contouring around a bump. At 4 miles, 5700 feet, begin heather and flower meadows with a spectacular view of Packwood Lake and Rainier. At 4½ miles the trail dips under cliffs and regains the ridge top, following to its very end at Johnson Peak.

Now a mile-long contour around the head of Lily Basin leads over several creeks (the first water of the trip) and a large rockslide. At 6 miles, 6100 feet, the path tops a ridge with magnificent views of Mt. Adams. Here, joined by the Angry Mountain trail, it contours a steep slope and drops to Heart Lake, 5700 feet, 6½ miles, the first logical campsite.

The trip can be extended—trail No. 86 continues to Jordan Basin, Goat Lake, and Snowgrass Flat (Hike 44).

Old road: 132   1323
New road: 48   48

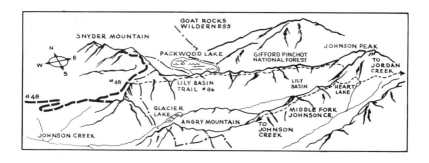

44 SNOWGRASS FLAT

**Round trip to Snowgrass Flat 8
  miles**
Hiking time 5 hours
High point 5700 feet

Elevation gain 1100 feet
Hikable July through November
One day or backpack
USGS Walupt Lake

One of the most famous meadows in the Cascades, a riot of color during
flower season. But when the flowers are gone the vast parklands higher
up, with views of Adams, St. Helens, and of course, the Goat Rocks, still
make the trip a genuine spectacular.

Drive US 12 south from Packwood 2.5 miles and turn east on Johnson
Creek road No. 21. At 15.7 miles turn left on road No. 2150 and at 18.5
miles turn left on road No. (2150)014, in 19 miles from Packwood coming
to Berry Patch and the trailhead, elevation 4600 feet.

Set out in the woods on Snowgrass Flat trail No. 96A, contouring the
slopes of Goat Ridge to a junction with trail No. 96 and then a crossing of
Goat Creek, 4700 feet. Especially in early summer, stop at the bridge to
apply insect repellent, lots of it, because from here the trail passes for ¼
mile through marshy forest where one may expect heavy attack by
swarms of mosquitoes.

At 2 miles the trail begins climbing from the valley bottom, leaving
behind the hordes of hungry bugs. At Bypass Camp, 3½ miles, cross
Snowgrass Creek and continue up, emerging occasionally from trees into
small meadows, and at 4 miles finally entering the open expanse of
Snowgrass Flat, 5700 feet.

Because of overgrazing by horses and punishment by heavy foot traffic,
and to give nature a chance to repair the damage, camping is no longer
permitted in the Flat; however, Bypass Camp is only minutes below and

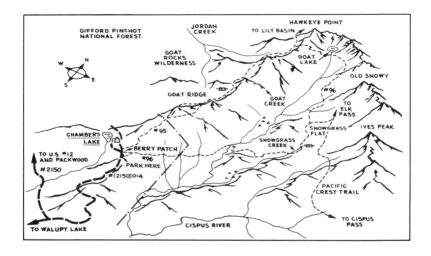

Snowgrass Flat from near Goat Lake

alpine camps a short way above, and either makes a fine base for exploratory walks. From the Flat hike another ½ mile and about 400 feet higher to join the Pacific Crest Trail. Campsites in the meadows here offer wide views, including all three southern volcanoes.

What to do now? For one choice, hike 2 miles south on the Crest Trail into the vast meadows of Cispus Basin and to Cispus Pass, 6473 feet, and superb views down the Klickitat River and out to 8201-foot Gilbert Peak.

Alternately, hike the Crest Trail north to its 7600-foot high point on the side of Old Snowy (Hike 45). Or, for a loop trip back to Berry Patch, total distance 13 miles, traverse to 6500-foot Goat Lake (sitting in a cold cirque and frozen most of most summers), and return by way of Goat Ridge.

The heaviest ashfall in an alpine area except on St. Helens itself buried the Snowgrass Flats vicinity in 1980. Few flowers bloomed that summer and much of the heather was killed. Paintbrush and lupine made a great show in 1981. It will be interesting to watch the meadows recover from the blast—as they have from many others of the like—and worse—over the centuries and eons.

| Old road: | 1302 | 1104 | 1118 |
| New road: | 21 | 2150 | (2150)014 |

45 GOAT ROCKS CREST

One-way trip 30 miles
Allow 3–4 days
High point 7600 feet
Elevation gain 5300 feet

Hikable July through September
USGS White Pass and Walupt
Lake

Walk a rock garden between heaven and earth on a narrow, 7000-foot ridge dividing Eastern and Western Washington. This spectacular section of the Pacific Crest Trail is popular with horse riders, so try it in the first half of July, when the tread is free enough of snow for safe hiking but not yet passable to horses; tiny alpine flowers are then in bloom, too. The climax portion can be done as a round trip of about 8 miles from Snowgrass Flat (Hike 44), but the route is described here in its full length from White Pass to Walupt Lake.

Drive to White Pass, elevation 4400 feet, and hike 7 miles south on the Pacific Crest Trail to Shoe Lake (Hike 39).

From Shoe Lake the trail crosses a low ridge and drops 900 feet into forest, then ascends and contours to Tieton Pass, 12 miles, and a junction with the North Fork Tieton River trail. Going only slightly up and down, the way proceeds on or near the crest to a Y at 13½ miles. The left (the old Crest Trail) contours 1 mile to a dead-end in McCall Basin, 5200 feet, with overused camps and much good off-trail exploring. The new Crest Trail steeply ascends 2 long miles to Elk Pass, 6600 feet. One great compensation for the energy output is that the entire way is in open country with views of Mt. Rainier and miles of meadowland on the slopes of Coyote Ridge to the west. The last campsites for 3½ miles are in flat meadows before the final drag to the pass, at which is a junction with the Coyote Ridge trail (Hike 42).

Views broaden at the pass—down to Packwood Lake and across the immense depth of Lake Creek to rugged Johnson Peak. The trail follows the ridge several hundred feet higher and then descends. From here one senses the quality of the route ahead. The tread can be seen—blasted out of cliffs, gouged in scree slopes; in some places the crest of the ridge has

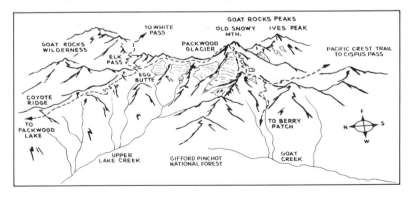

Mount Rainier and Coyote Ridge

actually been leveled off to give walking room.

The next 2 miles are mostly above 7000 feet, the highest Washington section of the Crest Trail and also the most dangerous. Meeting a horse party is bad business, because the horses cannot be turned around and thus hikers must backtrack to a safe turnout. Snowstorms can be expected in any month. Two parties of recent years have lost a member from hypothermia and there have been several narrow escapes. Don't attempt this section in poor weather.

The trail first contours and climbs to a 7100-foot point with a view of weird-shaped towers and small glaciers on 8201-foot Gilbert Peak, highest in the Goat Rocks. There is also a fine view of Old Snowy, 7930 feet. Nooks and crannies hold the superb rock gardens, which are in full bloom during early July.

The way now follows ups and downs of the narrow crest, sometimes on the exact top and other times swinging around small knobs. From a spot a little beyond the lowest portion, it is possible to avoid a climb by contouring across the Packwood Glacier and rejoining the trail where several signs can be seen in a saddle on the skyline. The glacier crossing is easy in July but by late August may involve hard ice; the best plan is to stay with the trail on its ascent to the highest elevation at 7600 feet on Old Snowy, a short sidetrip away from the 7930-foot summit.

The trail now descends. At 6900 feet is a rock shelter built by the Bellevue Presbyterian Church in memory of Dana May Yelverton, who died of exposure on the crest August 4, 1962. Winter snows have been hard on the building, which seems fated for early collapse.

From the cabin the path drops into parkland, at 21 miles intersecting the Snowgrass Flat trail (Hike 44), then contouring into the glory of Cispus Basin. The route continues in meadows to the Nannie Ridge trail at 24 miles, and then by this trail 6 miles to Walupt Lake, as described in Hike 47.

46 COLEMAN WEEDPATCH

Round trip 9 miles
Hiking time 6 hours
High point 5712 feet
Elevation gain 1900 feet

Hikable early July through
October
One day
USGS Walupt Lake

A grand viewpoint keeps the head turning around and around—from Adams to Rainier to the Goat Rocks, and down 1800 feet to tiny boats on Walupt Lake.

Drive toward Walupt Lake (Hike 47) but 3.2 miles from road No. 21—1.4 miles shy of the lake—find Coleman Weedpatch trail No. 121, elevation 3800 feet.

The first 1½ miles of trail ascend gently in forest, gaining a mere 400 feet. The last 1½ miles tilt, gaining 1000 feet to intersect the Pacific Crest Trail at 5200 feet. Here continuous forest yields to a mosaic of subalpine tree clumps and little heather-blueberry meadows, the living foreground contrasting with tree-framed glimpses of glaciers of Mt. Adams just 11 miles distant.

Turn north on the Crest Trail an easy 1½ miles to a bluff at 5712 feet. This is the place to unpack the lunch and soak in the scenery and speculate whether the fishermen on Walupt Lake are having any luck. Moving about the bluff gives unrestricted views of Adams.

But, you ask, where is the promised Weedpatch? It can be spotted, a green and squishy meadow-marsh 500 feet below, and should you descend you'll find all the weeds are flowers. However, you likely won't descend because from the bluff the Crest Trail is in forest, no views, for 4 miles.

Old road: 1114
New road: 2160

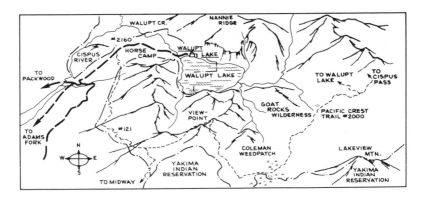

47 NANNIE RIDGE

Round trip to Nannie Peak 7 miles	**Round trip to Sheep Lake 12 miles**
Hiking time 4½ hours	**Hiking time 8 hours**
High point 5800 feet	**High point 5710 feet**
Elevation gain 1800 feet	**Elevation gain 2300 feet**
Hikable July through September	**Hikable late July through**
One day	**September**
USGS Walupt Lake	**One day or backpack**

A long hike through meadowland to a small lake, then on for views to the head of the Klickitat River and up to the rugged pinnacles of 8201-foot Gilbert Peak, highest in the Goat Rocks; or an easy day hike to Nannie Peak, overlooking meadows and summits of the Goat Rocks.

Drive US 12 south from Packwood 2.5 miles and turn east on Johnson Creek road No. 21. At 18.5 miles (from Packwood) turn left on road No. 2160. At 20.5 miles the good logging road turns off and No. 2160 continues to Walupt Lake at 24 miles, elevation 3927 feet. Find the trailhead in the Walupt Lake Picnic Area.

Start on trail No. 101 and in a few yards turn left on Nannie Ridge trail No. 98 and begin to climb. The first 1½ miles are through timber, passing two small streams—the last water for 3 miles. At about 2 miles the trees thin out; the next mile is miserably rutted. At about 3 miles the way tops a 5600-foot ridge. On the very crest an unmarked, unmaintained, but quite decent trail climbs in ½ mile to Nannie Peak, 6106 feet, site of a former lookout. The summit is a ¼-mile ridge of heather, grass, alpine trees, and rocks. Be sure to explore the full length—from the south end are views of Adams and St. Helens and from the north end views of Gilbert Peak and vast meadows.

Those who choose the longer trip now must lose a discouraging 300 feet as the main trail drops under cliffs. At 3½ miles is a pond (which may dry up in late summer) and another trail, also unmarked, switchbacking to

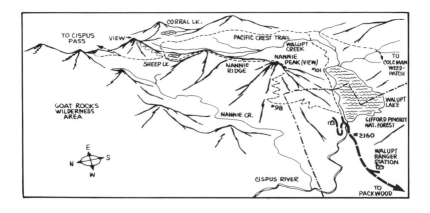

Mount Adams and Sheep Lake

the summit of Nannie Peak. A short bit beyond the pond look down on a small lake, about 500 feet below the trail, a tempting place to camp. After passing below more cliffs of Nannie, the way regains the ridge and meadow country and follows ups and downs of the crest to lovely little Sheep Lake, 5¾ miles, 5710 feet, surrounded by grass and flowers, an ideal camp. The best sites are on the ridge to the west beside a row of protecting trees. Walk around the shore for views of Adams and St. Helens.

A visit to a viewpoint above the Klickitat River is mandatory. There are two choices. For one, hike the ridge almost directly north a long mile to its summit at 6512 feet. The other alternative is to find the Pacific Crest Trail on the north side of the lake and follow it northward 1½ miles to where it crosses a small pass into Klickitat drainage. For a return follow the Crest Trail south and take trail No. 101 back to the starting point.

Johnson Creek road—Old:	1302	Old road:	1114
New:	21	New road:	2160

Small tarn near Pacific Crest Trail

48 WALUPT CREEK LOOP

Loop trip 14 miles
Allow 2 days
High point 5710 feet

Elevation gain 1800 feet
Hikable July through October
USGS Walupt Lake

The loop begins in lovely forest beside a scenic lake, ascends to alpine meadows and cirque lakes and broad views from an old fire lookout site, and concludes with a magnificent ridge ramble. A choice of good camps provides a happy night between two happy days.

Drive to Walupt Lake Campground (Hike 47) and find trail No. 101, elevation 3950 feet. A few hundred feet along it is the junction with trail No. 98, the return route.

The first 2 miles are pure joy, the trail following the mile-long lake with modest ups and downs and continuing in valley forests to a bridge over Walupt Creek, 4040 feet. The next 1 mile is pure agony, climbing 600 feet in relentless switchbacks. But the angle moderates to a gentler, nonzigzag ascent of subalpine parkland, through the trees and over the flowers, at one point skirting a deep gully with an excellent view of Gilbert Peak. At 3¾ miles is the first nice place for a night, Short Trail Camp, on the banks of a stream. A bit beyond beside a tiny lake is another camp.

At 4 miles intersect the Pacific Crest Trail at 5000 feet. Turn north, climbing to steep meadows, looking over your shoulder to 6660-foot Lakeview Mountain and Mt. Adams. After a mile of flowers and views the way enters woods with only occasional windows out.

At 7½ miles from the road the Crest Trail comes to the second set of good camps at the crossing of Walupt Creek, 5500 feet. At 8 miles is Sheep Lake, limited camping. Here find the junction with trail No. 98, route of the sky-high return along Nannie Ridge (Hike 47).

Old road: 1114
New road: 2160

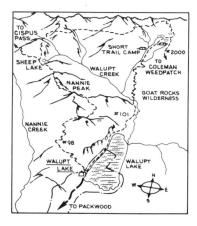

49 NORWAY PASS

Round trip 5 miles
Hiking time 3 hours
High point 4508 feet
Elevation gain 900 feet

Hikable July through September
One day
USGS Spirit Lake

Here is the place to appreciate the devastation of May 1980, and to view the new (and ghostly) Spirit Lake and the crater blasted from the former perfect symmetry of the "Fujiyama of the West." Wear sturdy shoes for wading through pumice. Carry water and be prepared for hot sun—there is no shade (no *trees*) on the trail.

Drive road No. 25 either 22 miles from Randle or 44 miles from Cougar and turn uphill on road No. 99, signed "Mt. St. Helens—Windy Ridge Viewpoint." At 8.9 miles from road No. 25 turn right on Ryan Lake road No. 26 and in 1 mile reach Norway Pass trailhead, elevation 3600 feet.

The trail ascends in switchbacks through fallen timber. Note that on slopes where the blast of hot gas and ash blew straight from the mountain the trees are blown flat in tidy parallel lines; where the blast eddied in the lee of a hill they are piled one atop the other in a haphazard jackstraw effect.

The feature of interest near the pass used to be the old mining machinery. It's still there, including a badly dented boiler, but the view, of course, is now the thing. Look down from the pass to Spirit Lake, half-filled with logs. Notice how a giant wave swept the slopes bare a thousand feet above the shore.

In 1986 the trail will be extended over Mt. Margaret to Johnston Ridge for even greater views, and more than 150 miles of trails are planned to be built in the monument eventually. Naturally, those plans are subject to change. 1980 wasn't the volcano's first blast, won't be its last.

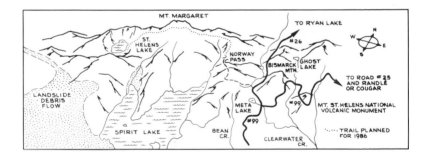

Spirit Lake and Mount St. Helens in 1982 (above), *and 1975* (below).

50 GOAT MOUNTAIN

Round trip to Deadman Lake 11
  miles
Hiking time 5½ hours
High point 5300 feet
Elevation gain 1900 feet in, 1000
  feet out

Hikable July through
  mid-October
One day or backpack
USGS Spirit Lake

One of the most exciting ridge walks in the South Cascades, through meadows of soft pumice spotted with flowers, huckleberry bushes, and alpine trees, by little spring-fed lakelets ringed by fields of grass to ¼-mile-wide Deadmans Lake surrounded by forest. Views south to the depths of the Green River valley, to the Mt. Margaret backcountry topped by Mt. St. Helens, and north out Quartz Creek valley to Mt. Rainier.

Drive south from the center of Randle on the road signed "Cispus, Mt. Adams, etc." Cross the Cowlitz River and at a junction in 1 mile keep straight on road No. 25. At 8.7 miles cross the Cispus River to a junction. Continue straight ahead on road No. 26, signed "Ryan Lake." At 22.5 miles from Randle turn right on road No. 2612 and at 22.8 miles find the trailhead, No. 217, just beyond the Ryan Lake parking area, elevation 3400 feet.

The trail begins with ¾ mile over the fairy level Devastated Area, steeply switchbacks in and out of the Blast Area, and at 1¾ miles, 4600 feet, tops the ridge which, by the chances of the eruption, escaped the catastrophe.

The way follows the ups and downs of the crest. At 2 miles the trail passes above the first of the lakelets, at 3 miles contours around a 5600-foot high point, and at 3¾ miles, 5200 feet, crosses from the south side of the ridge to the north, directly above two more lakelets. Now begins a descent of 900 feet to Deadmans Lake, 5½ miles, a wonderful spot for a basecamp. The trail can be followed another 2¾ miles to 4948-foot Vanson Peak, site of a former lookout; a sidetrip leads to Vanson Lake.

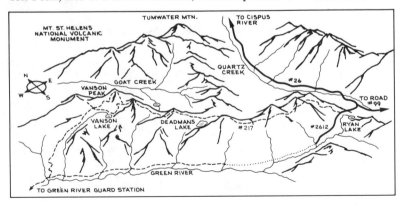

Mount Rainier and tarn on Goat Mountain

Old road: 125   115
New road: 25   26

Langille Peak and Mount Rainier

CISPUS RIVER
Dark Divide—Unprotected area

LANGILLE RIDGE—
McCOY PEAK

**One-way trip to Boundary Trail 11
  miles**
Allow 1–2 days
High point 5200 feet
**Elevation gain 3800 feet, loss 1400
  feet**

Hikable July through October
One day or backpack
**USGS McCoy Peak and Tower
  Rock**

An 11-mile ridge of forests, flowers, crags, and views extends from the confluence of McCoy and Yellow Jacket Creeks to Boundary Trail No. 1. The hiking route largely avoids the ridge crest, a series of cliffs and peaks, going up and down to dodge both. Only parts of the trail are shown on the USGS maps; rest assured it's there, and has been a long time. Carry water; the only year-round source is Bear Creek.

Three trails give access to the ridge, all steep in spots, and often deep in sand that is replenished every century or so by a generous Mt. St. Helens. The ridge can be sampled from either end or, if transportation can be arranged, done one way; in this case logic dictates starting at the higher end, the Boundary Trail. For the shortest route to the old lookout site on McCoy Peak, take the Rough trail.

Begin the approach to all three trails by driving south from Randle 1 mile, turning left on road No. 23, in 9 miles (from Randle) turning right on road No. 28, and at 10 miles coming to the junction with road No. 29.

Rough trail access: Take road No. 29 for 10.2 miles and turn right .5 mile on road No. (29000)115 to Rough trail No. 283, elevation 2600 feet.

The trail isn't actually rough on the feet but surely is on leg muscles and wind as it gains 2000 feet in 2 miles to intersect the Langille Ridge trail No. 259 at 4600 feet. Go right, losing 250 feet to cross Bear Creek, and climb to tiny Grasshopper Lake (a puddle), 5086 feet. At the junction here go left, climbing to the top of McCoy Peak, 5856 feet, about 4½ miles from the road.

Boundary Trail access: Take road No. 29 for 15.1 miles to the crossing of Boundary Trail No. 1, elevation 3900 feet.

Hike the Boundary Trail westward, gaining 500 feet in 2 miles to the Langille Ridge trail. Turn north 11 miles to road No. 2809.

Northern access: Continue on road No. 28 another 7.8 miles and turn left 2.6 miles on road No. 2809 to Langille Ridge trail No. 259, elevation 2600 feet.

The trail begins on an abandoned logging road; look sharp to spot the start of true trail. In long switchbacks the way ascends to a 3500-foot wooded ridge and continues climbing around slopes of Langille Peak, attaining the crest of the ridge at 5200 feet. The trail loses 300 feet, sidehilling and climbing to Grasshopper "Puddle," 5086 feet, 5¼ miles. South of the lake an unmaintained path ascends McCoy Peak, the summit 6 miles from the road.

From the lake, Langille Ridge trail loses 800 feet to campsites at the Bear Creek crossing and climbs 250 feet to the junction with Rough trail. The way continues climbing another 200 feet, then drops 300 feet to go under a cliff, and finally regains the ridge crest, which it holds most of the remaining way to the junction with Boundary Trail No. 1 at 11 miles. To finish the trip you must, of course, walk 2 more miles to road No. 29, for a trip total of 13 miles.

Old road:	123	112	112A	111
New road:	23	28	2810	29

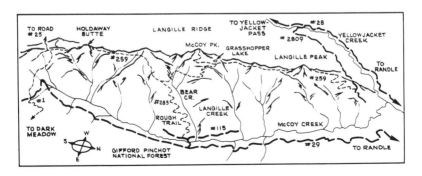

Mount Adams from Juniper Ridge

CISPUS RIVER
Dark Divide—Unprotected area

52   JUNIPER RIDGE

Round trip to Juniper Peak 8 miles
Hiking time 5 hours
High point 5593 feet
Elevation gain 2000 feet
Hikable mid-June through November
One day
USGS McCoy Peak

Round trip to Boundary Trail 26 miles
Allow 3 days
High point about 5788 feet
Elevation gain 2300 feet, plus ups and downs
Hikable July through October

Dramatic views up the Cispus River to Mt. Adams, out to Mt. Rainier and Mt. St. Helens, and over endless forested hills and valleys—all while walking a long ridge, sometimes on open hillsides covered with huckleberries, sometimes in young forest just getting established after the tremendous Cispus fires of 1902 and 1918. The route provides a variety of trips: an easy afternoon stroll to a 4500-foot saddle (the trail this far generally is free of snow in early or mid-June); a day hike to Juniper Peak; an overnight backpack; or a long approach to the Boundary Trail (Hike 56).

Turn south in Randle, cross the Cowlitz River, and drive 1 mile. Turn left on road No. 23 and in 9 miles (from Randle) turn right on road No. 28. At 10 miles leave pavement and go straight ahead on road No. 29. In 14 miles turn left on road No. 2904 and at 18 miles find the trailhead, elevation about 3500 feet.

The trail goes a few hundred feet through a clearcut, enters second-growth forest, and climbs under two prominent knolls, ascending steadily, with frequent views, 2¼ miles to a 4500-foot saddle. The trail continues climbing, gaining 1100 feet to within a few feet of the top of 5593-foot Juniper Peak (4 miles, a good turnaround for day hikers), then, dropping about 400 feet, goes under cliffs. At 5½ miles is a super-great huckleberry patch—outstanding even in an area famous for huckleberries. At 5¾ miles pass a tiny lake and campsites.

At 7 miles is the Sunrise Peak trail, a ¼-mile sidetrip up a steep stairway with handrails to the 5880-foot site of a former lookout; by the junction is a fair camp. At 7¾ miles, on a big saddle in the ridge, is Old Cow Camp with water and scenic camping. The trail again drops several hundred feet and passes under cliffs of 5788-foot Jumbo Peak, 9 miles, then descends to Dark Meadow, 12 miles, 4300 feet, offering plenty of water and campsites. From here a trail drops 3½ miles to road No. 23.

From Dark Meadow the trail proceeds ¾ mile to good campsites in a large basin and in ¼ mile more reaches the Boundary Trail at a point 2 miles from the road at McCoy Pass.

Note the many sawn stumps along the ridge to Juniper. These are not from logging but the cutting of snags, which in the old Smoky Bear Dogma had to be eliminated lest they draw lightning and flame like torches. Contemporary foresters know that snags are the feeding and nesting headquarters of many important birds.

Old road:	123	112	111	1106
New road:	23	28	29	2904

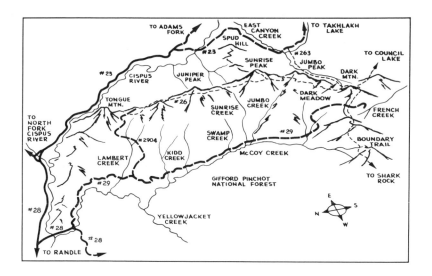

53 TONGUE MOUNTAIN

Round trip 4 miles
Hiking time 3 hours
High point 4750 feet
Elevation gain 1300 feet

Hikable late June through
September
One day
USGS Tower Rock

The Cispus River twists and turns through the forest 3000 feet beneath your toes, Rainier and Adams loom big and icy in the distance, and the perfumes of the flowers overpower the reek of your sardine sandwiches. The rocky jut of Tongue Mountain from the north end of Juniper Ridge once was the site of a fire lookout, sufficient recommendation.

Drive to the Juniper Peak trailhead (Hike 52), elevation 3500 feet. (Juniper Peak has bigger views and more wildflowers, but this hike takes about half the time and energy, a real bargain.)

Find Tongue Mountain trail No. 294 on the north side of the road and set out in second-growth forest dating from the early 1930s, gaining 500 feet in an easy up-and-down mile to a junction. The straight-ahead fork drops 5 miles to the Cispus River; go right, uphill. Short switchbacks ascend a rock garden of blue lupine and penstemon, yellow wallflower, and orange paintbrush, at 2 miles topping out in a saddle, 4750 feet. Views, flowers, the spot to open the sardine can.

The horses that used to carry supplies for the lookout cabin atop Tongue Mountain, 4838 feet, stopped here, and so should you. The footpath the final hundred feet to the summit long since has slid out, leaving a rock scramble very simple for a climber, but for a hiker, one false move and he's in the Cispus River, or near.

Old road: 123   112   111   1106
New road: 23   28   29   2904

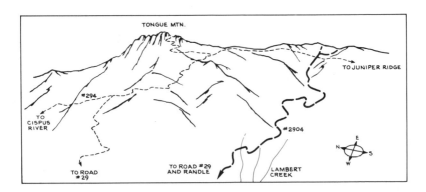

Tongue Mountain and Mount Rainier from Juniper Ridge

54 DARK MEADOW

Round trip 4 miles
Hiking time 3 hours
High point 4800 feet
Elevation gain 900 feet
Hikable early July through
   October
One day
USGS McCoy Peak

Round trip 8 miles
Allow 2 days
Elevation gain 900 feet in, 400 feet
   out

Who cannot yearn to find what Boundary Trail No. 1 is all about? Here is a pleasant sampling—flowers in summer, the blue of lupine, the red of paintbrush, the red-yellow of columbine, the orange of tiger lily, the white-yellow of aster and daisy, and the startling (on this side of the Cascades) scarlet of gilia. And tall huckleberry bushes to keep in mind for the pie-making season in fall. Day hikers can have lunch at a good viewpoint. Overnighters may proceed to Dark Creek, which flows at least half the summer. Sights and sounds of clearcutting never are far away; all the more reason for saving a remnant of virgin forest in the proposed Dark Divide Wilderness.

From Randle drive roads Nos. 23, 28, and 29 to the crossing of Boundary Trail No. 1 (Hike 51, "Boundary Trail access"), elevation 3900 feet.

Find the trail on the left side of the road and climb steadily in old virgin forest ⅓ mile to the start of forest that also is virgin (*not* "second growth," a term that implies human harvesting) but young, dating from a 1918 fire. Note that the farther the trail proceeds into the burn the more the trees thin out and give way to huckleberries and flowers, an example of the way higher-elevation forests regenerate: slow invasion inward from surviving forests that protect tender seedlings from freezing in winter and baking in summer. Despite the plain evidence offered by such burns as this, government foresters only recently have officially admitted that in such sites genuine "tree farming" demands small patch

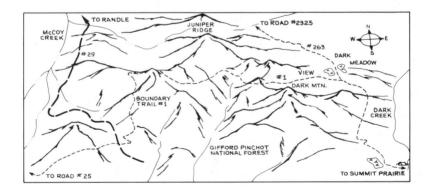

Dark Meadow and Mount Adams

cuts, not the horizon-to-horizon clearcuts of the tree-mining free enterprisers.

At 1½ miles the trail dips, climbs to the saddle between Dark Mountain and Juniper Ridge, and at 2 miles attains the ridge crest and the viewpoint, 4800 feet. Look out *there* to Adams, *there* to the Goat Rocks, and then away from ice and rocks, down to Dark Meadow, actually a bright green.

If hauling a stone on the back, and seeking a night's home for it, follow the Boundary Trail down 400 feet in ¾ mile to Dark Meadow and traverse the north side of Dark Mountain 1½ miles more to Dark Creek and (possibly) water, 4300 feet.

To sample the Boundary Trail more fully, stick with it to Summit Prairie, 6 miles from road No. 29 (Hike 56).

Old road: 123   112   111
New road: 23   28   29

Juniper Ridge from top of Summit Prairie

55 SUMMIT PRAIRIE

Round trip 8½ miles
Hiking time 4 hours
High point 5238 feet
Elevation gain 1000 feet

Hikable mid-July through
  October
One day
USGS East Canyon Ridge

So, a person hikes to the highest point of Quartz Creek Ridge, finds himself on a wooded knoll, and complains, "Where's the prairie?" Now, one must keep in mind there were a lot of jokers in the backcountry in the ancient past. Did a gang of them, after laboriously whacking down trees to clear ground for a fire-lookout cabin, sardonically put "prairie" on the 1926 map? Or was the knoll then, in the aftermath of the Little Ice Age, veritably a meadow, since invaded by trees? Probably both.

Drive road No. 23 some 33 miles from Randle (Hike 56) or 23 miles from Trout Lake to a scant mile south of Baby Shoe Pass and go off on road No. 2334. In 1 mile pass Council Lake Campground and at 3.3 miles turn right on a primitive road 4 miles to trail No. 1A, signed "Boundary Trail ½ mile," elevation 4150 feet.

The ½ mile leads to the Boundary Trail (Hike 56). Turn left on it to countour (upsy-downsy) below cliffs of Table Mountain, gaining (netting) 600 feet in 3 miles.

At 4 miles go left on trail No. 2 a steep ¼ mile to the old lookout site, 5238 feet. That big white volcano to the north is Rainier. The one to the east is Adams. The one to the south, in a foreign state, is Hood. To the west are Juniper Ridge and peaks of the Boundary Trail route. Go soon, before invading trees wipe out the remnant of prairie, not to be recleared until the next Ice Age, or forest fire.

Old road: 123 N925
New road: 23 2334

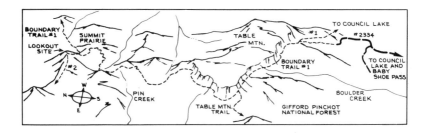

56 BOUNDARY TRAIL

One-way trip 37 miles	Hikable July through October
Allow 4–6 days	USGS Spirit Lake, French Butte,
High point 5000 feet	McCoy Peak, Steamboat
Elevation gain about 4700 feet	Mountain

A National Scenic Trail (so designated in 1979) eventually will start at Mt. Adams, follow the crest of the Lewis River–Cispus River watershed, and finish at Mt. St. Helens. Currently, part of the way near Adams lies along roads, but 37 miles are complete. At six places roads cut the route, which therefore can be traveled in small sections if desired. The final stretch suffered a serious accident in 1980. For a good sample of the country, hike from McCoy Creek to Elk Pass.

The hike can be taken in either direction, depending on whether one prefers to watch Adams or St. Helens grow larger and the other smaller. The east-to-west direction is described here.

Turn south in Randle, cross the Cowlitz River, and in 1 mile turn left. Follow road No. 23 over Baby Shoe Pass and at 33 miles from Randle keep right on road No. 2334 a final 1 mile to Council Lake Campground, elevation 4200 feet.

The way starts with a steep climb up the abandoned Council Bluff road, then gradually drops to a stream crossing at 4½ miles and again goes up. At 6¾ miles round Table Mountain, at 8½ miles pass Prairie Mountain and a good camp, climb a few hundred feet, and drop to campsites near Dark Meadow. Climb again to a 4000-foot saddle at 12 miles and descend to McCoy Creek road No. 29, 14½ miles, 3800 feet. At 15½ miles are more camps in a basin south of the trail, which then rises steadily to 16½ miles. A bit beyond, keep left on new tread ascending to a 4800-foot viewpoint, 17 miles, then skirting below impressive cliffs of

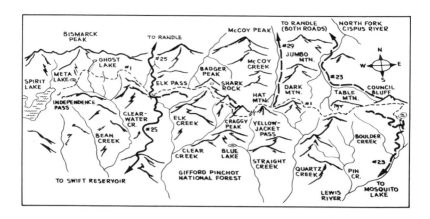

Mount Adams from side of Hat Mountain

Hat Rock while dropping to 4000-foot Yellowjacket Pass; campsites here a few feet to the south.

At 21½ miles pass under 4800-foot Craggy Peak, next under Shark Rock, and with little change in elevation contour slopes of 5659-foot Badger Peak to Badger Lake, 25½ miles; numerous good camps. At 29½ miles reach Mosquito Meadows. The trail continues, crossing road No. 25 at Elk Pass, 3900 feet, 30½ miles.

The scene is, of course, increasingly dramatic as modifications of the pre-1980 landscape are neared. The trail enters timber, emerges into a clearcut, and follows a spur road ¼ mile before reverting to footpath and trees. At 33½ miles the route again strikes a road/jeep track and goes along it almost 2 miles, crossing a stream at 34½ miles and at 35½ miles coming to Mt. St. Helens road No. 99 at Bear Meadow Viewpoint.

Here, for now, the Boundary Trail ends–having once continued another 8 miles through the Blast Zone to Spirit Lake. In the near future it will be extended around Strawberry Mountain to a new terminus at the Norway Pass trailhead (Hike 49).

| Old road: | 123 | 111 | 125 | 100 |
| New road: | 23 | 29 | 25 | 99 |

57 QUARTZ CREEK

**Round trip to Quartz Creek Camp
9 miles
Hiking time 7 hours
High point 2500 feet
Elevation gain 500 feet, plus
  innumerable ups and downs**

**Hikable June through November
One day or backpack
USGS Quartz Creek (trail not
  shown)**

Trees 3 and 4 feet in diameter, and even 8, line the trail, rising straight without a limb for 100 feet, a magnificent example of an increasingly rare ecosystem—the virgin lowland forest. But take the hike as soon as possible because these are probably among the best saw logs remaining in Gifford Pinchot National Forest, and notices of timber sales are tacked to trees for almost 4 miles. The creek usually is out of sight in a deep canyon but never out of sound. Three stream crossings add excitement.

Drive 17.5 miles from Pine Creek Visitors Center, a the north end of Swift Reservoir, up Lewis River road No. 90 to the Quartz Creek bridge and trail No. 5, elevation 1800 feet. (If the logging road is open, one could follow roads Nos. 9346 and 9343 and bypass the first 2 miles of trail and two of the stream crossings, but this also would bypass some of the finest trees.)

The trail is seldom level, repeatedly climbing steeply over an obstacle and dropping just as steeply. The first ⅔ mile is along the river on an ancient miner's road, the trees here as yet unmolested. At the end of the road is the ancient miner's rusted machinery and the first interesting stream crossing, of Platinum Creek, difficult when the water is high.

The way climbs steeply, traverses a clearcut (credit is due the Forest Service for keeping the trail open during cutting operations and, when necessary, rebuilding it) and at 2 miles comes to Straight Creek. A large log with ax-flattened top spans the flood; a nervous person might feel better scooting across in a sitting position. On the far side is a good camp and just downstream are Quartz Creek Falls; other falls are upstream on Straight Creek.

The trail ascends a clearcut and at 2½ miles reenters forest, coming at 4 miles to Snagtooth Creek, another log bridge, and more camps. At about 4½ miles is an unsigned junction. The main trail, marked by two

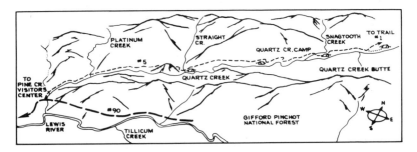

Crossing Snagtooth Creek

blazes, goes left, uphill. Take the right, marked by four slash-line blazes, and drop ¼ mile to delightful Quartz Creek Camp, surrounded by magnificent trees, 2300 feet.

Quartz Creek trail continues. At 6 miles is a junction with the Snagtooth Mountain trail leading to road No. 9341. At 10½ miles the way intersects Boundary Trail No. 1 near road No. 2325.

Old road: N90
New road: 90

Lewis River near Bolt Camp

LEWIS RIVER
Dark Divide—Unprotected area

LEWIS RIVER

One-way trip 9½ miles
Hiking time 6 hours
High point 1600 feet
Elevation gain 1000 feet upstream,
  600 feet downstream

Hikable March through
  November
One day or backpack
USGS Burnt Peak and Spencer
  Butte

A forest of huge firs, cedars, and maples serves as a canopy to a green and varied carpet of Oregon-grape, vanilla leaf, moss dotted with oxalis, and shoulder-high shrubs. The Forest Service has promised to preserve in a natural condition a wide corridor along the Lewis River, keeping this trail—perhaps the last low-elevation valley path remaining in Gifford Pinchot National Forest—as an 11-mile sample and reminder of the many, many miles of such splendor that we inherited and that are now mostly gone.

The trail can be hiked in either direction, and parties that can arrange transportation to allow a one-way trip would be well-advised to start at the top, which is 400 feet higher than the bottom. However, parties making a round trip should start at the bottom and thus be sure to cover at least the lower 3 miles, where the best trees are; for this reason the bottom-to-top direction is described here.

From road No. 25 at the end of Swift Reservoir turn right on road No. 90. At 5.2 miles turn left on road No. 9039, and at 6.2 miles cross the Lewis River at the Crab Creek bridge. At 6.6 miles find the lower trailhead, elevation about 1100 feet.

To reach the upper trailhead, from the junction of roads Nos. 90 and 9093 continue on No. 90 to a concrete bridge over the Lewis River at 14.5 miles from the ranger station. A few yards from the west end of the bridge find the trailhead, elevation about 1400 feet.

From the lower beginning, trail No. 31 immediately drops to river level, about 1000 feet, and magnificent forest. The way winds along bottomland flats, climbs a small bank, and emerges into an old clearcut at 1 mile. To somewhat beyond 1½ miles the path follows the margin of the logging before reentering virgin trees. After a few steep ups and downs, at just under 2½ miles, is Bolt Camp; the shelter here is amazingly well-preserved considering it was built in the early 1930s. (In 1979 a Forest Service employee spent his days off reshaking the cabin.) At 4 miles the valley narrows to a canyon, a good turnaround for round-trip hikers, since from this point the trail goes up and down a lot but never again reaches river level—though there are several spots where one can easily drop to the stream.

At 7 miles the trail climbs a 300-foot bluff. At 7½ miles find a viewpoint a few feet off the tread and look down to the canyon sliced in columnar basalt. From here on, the river is unseen and old forest yields to young forest dating from the Spencer Butte fire which swept the area in the 1920s; because snags were then considered a major fire hazard, most were cut many years ago. At 9 miles cross Cussed Hollow and climb over the last bump to the upper trailhead at 9½ miles, 1400 feet.

That's the main hike. A new-built stretch of trail goes on. Cross road No. 90 and walk 1¾ miles to Lower Lewis River Falls, a splendid cataract. In ¼ mile more is Lower Falls Campground.

| Old road: | 125 | N90 | N836 |
| New road: | 25 | 90 | 9039 |

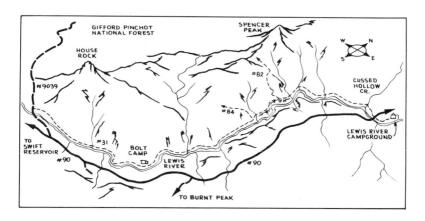

59 SHARK ROCK AND CRAGGY PEAK

Round trip to Boundary Trail 13 miles
Hiking time 5 hours
High point 5200 feet
Elevation gain 1800 feet

Hikable mid-July through early November
One day or backpack
USGS Spencer Butte, Quartz Creek, McCoy Peak

Follow a wooded ridge to a mountain lake, 2 miles of alpine meadows, and views, and views, and views. Nowhere else in the State of Washington can one see so vast an expanse of solid virgin forest as in the vista over Straight Creek and Quartz Creek to Mt. Adams; only a few distant clearings far to the south break the solid green. (Underfoot, though, is a good bit of gray: the Big St. Helens Show of 1980 dropped 6–8 inches of ash hereabouts, mostly popcorn-size.) Try this trip early in July; if conditions are right, there may be miles of beargrass in bloom.

The trail is harassed by machines and jeopardized by logging, including a timber sale ¼ mile from Blue Lake. That the path has survived until now is due solely to a Sierra Club lawsuit—now withdrawn as a condition of the 1984 Washington Wilderness Act. Logging at these high elevations is particularly shocking because the timber has relatively little commercial value—a quarter or more of the trees are left on the ground to rot after being cut and a new forest may be 150–300 years growing.

From Lewis River Ranger Station on Swift Reservoir, drive north on road No. 25 (passing a junction with road No. 92). At 5.6 miles turn right on road No. 93. Watch all intersections carefully; during logging operations some sideroads are used more than the main road. At 18.7 miles find the trailhead, elevation 3400 feet.

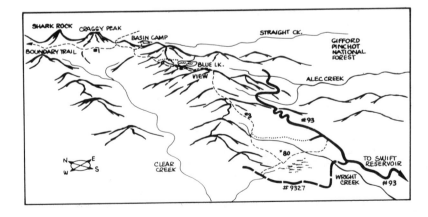

Blue Lake and Mount Adams

The way starts as trail No. 80, part of the old Spirit Lake—Guler trail. In 1½ up-and-down miles reach an intersection (only ¼ mile from road No. 93, a possible shortcut) with trail No. 3, signed "Blue Lake." Follow this trail uphill. At 2½ miles pass close to a clearcut which offers another shortcut. (To reach this alternative starting point from the trailhead, drive road No. 9327 another 1.3 miles to an unmarked spur and find your way across the clearing.)

In the next 2 miles the trail climbs gently, eventually ascending a wide ridge. At a little over 4½ miles the ridge becomes quite narrow and at times the route is steep. But the vista begins. At 5200 feet the way contours around a high point and drops to a view of Blue Lake at 5 miles. (To get to 4553-foot Blue Lake hike the trail to the point where the lake comes clearly in sight and find an unmarked way trail down to the shore.)

The timber thins, the trail enters meadows, and at 5½ miles, 5200 feet, is a short sidetrail to a campsite—water is scarce after the snow melts. At 6 miles pass a sidetrail ¼ mile southeast to Basin Camp. After contouring slopes of a knob, at 6½ miles, 5200 feet, join trail No. 1, the Boundary Trail (Hike 56).

For the widest views along the route, wander up either of the grassy knolls at 3½ or 4 miles. Shark Rock at the head of Clear Creek is the most impressive rocky peak on the Boundary Ridge.

Old road:	125	N92	N920	Lewis River road—Old:	N923
New road:	25	92	9327	New:	93

60 BADGER PEAK

Round trip 10 miles
Hiking time 7 hours
High point 5664 feet
Elevation gain 1600 feet

Hikable late July through
September
One day or backpack
USGS French Butte

The Forest Service blasted off the top of the peak to make a flat space for a fire-lookout cabin. The cabin is gone, and a lot of the forests it was there to help protect, but the views haven't quit. South is Mt. Hood, east are Mt. Adams and jagged crags of Shark Rock Scenic Area, north is Mt. Rainier, and west is a close-up look of the smoldering remains of Mt. St. Helens. However, the hike is not unmixed glee because loggers are working both sides of the route, a forested ridge, and if wilderness protection is not obtained, they eventually will clearcut the trail. Further, much of the tread is 6 inches deep in 1980 pumice, as slow going as dry sand. Finally, hikers not equipped with ice ax and knowledge of how to use it must not attempt the peak in early summer, when a dangerous snow gully blocks the trail near the summit.

Drive road No. 25 to Elk Pass, 24 miles from Randle, 40 miles from Cougar, and find Boundary Trail No. 1. The trailhead is hidden in the woods about 200 feet north of the junction of roads Nos. 25 and 2551, elevation 4080 feet.

The trail sets out along ups and downs of the ridge crest, at 2 miles passing trail No. 292, this junction 1 mile from road No. 28, an alternate starting point. The way ascends across ridge slopes to a junction at 4 miles, several hundred feet from Badger Lake, 4940 feet. Campsites here rely on the lake for water, to be kept in mind should you be of a mind to take a swim.

The summit of Badger Peak is a scant 1 mile from the lake. To get there, climb from the junction in soft pumice, contouring a steep slope just below the ridge crest, and join trail No. 257 (from road No. 2816).

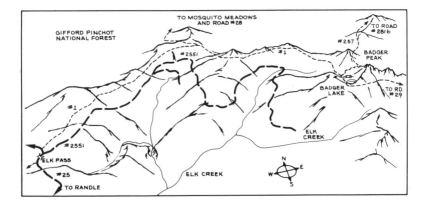

Streams of smoke formed by 60 m.p.h. wind. Taken from Badger Mountain

(Two game traces as good as the built trail also ascend this ridge.) Just below the summit is a steep gully, unworthy of notice when snow free, but when full, one slip and you're 300 feet down the mountain, battering the boulders.

Aside from that, simply remember to beware of active volcanoes.

Old road: 125
New road: 25

61 ADAMS CREEK MEADOWS

Round trip 8 miles
Hiking time 6 hours
High point 6840 feet
Elevation gain 2300 feet

Hikable mid-July through
mid-October
One day or backpack
USGS Mt. Adams West and Green
Mountain

A grand place it is to sit, gazing to Goat Rocks, Rainier, the truncated cone of St. Helens, and the plumes of steam and ash that go unreported in the press now that everybody's grown casual about having an active volcano in the neighborhood. Green forest ridges (moth-eaten by clearcuts) contrast with gray ridges that were in the main-line 1980 blast. A great place it is to camp, too, for the sunsets and sunrises, the seas of valley clouds, the swirls of storm clouds arriving from the ocean, and, at night, the monstrous skyglow of Puget Sound City. A superb place it is to roam, also, among raw moraines and blocky lava flows, by ponds and waterfalls, past fields of flowers under the Forgotten Giant, the Adams Glacier, tumbling a vertical mile from the summit to the edge of the gardens.

From the center of Randle, take the road signed "Mt. Adams" and drive a scant mile south to a split. Veer left on road No. 23, signed "Cispus Center, Mt. Adams, Trout Lake, Cispus Road." Stay on road No. 23, paved at first, then gravel, to 32 miles from Randle. Turn left on road No. 2329. In 2 miles pass the sideroad to Takhlakh Lake and at 5.7 miles

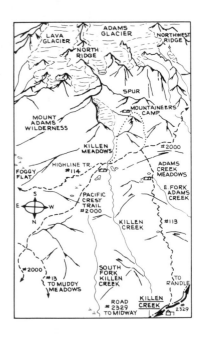

Mount Adams and meadow

Wind-sculptured tree and Mount Adams

(37.7 miles from Randle) find the parking area and trailhead, elevation 4584 feet.

Killen Creek trail No. 113 (which never goes near Killen Creek) enters the Mt. Adams Wilderness, ascends open pine forest brightly flowered by beargrass in early summer, and at 2½ miles, 5840 feet, opens out in a broad meadow brilliant with shooting star, avalanche lily, and marsh marigold early on, later with paintbrush and heather, cinquefoil and phlox. Here is the first water, East Fork Adams Creek, and nice camps before and around ruins of an old cabin.

The trail ascends lava-flow steps to intersect and end at the Pacific Crest Trail, 3 miles, 6084 feet. Beyond here is only a foot path.

Above the trail intersection uprises a spur ridge that ultimately joins the North Cleaver, a customary route to the summit of Adams. At 1 long mile from the Crest Trail is a broad meadow swale at 6840 feet in the crest of this ridge, called High Camp, Mountaineers Camp, Adams Glacier Camp, take your pick. There are two approaches. The most popular is to turn north ¼ mile on the Crest Trail, round the base of the spur ridge, and turn uphill through meadows and rockslides of Killen Meadows to a culminating snowfield. Seemingly more complicated but actually easier, all steep snow dodgeable, is to go south a bit on the Crest Trail and turn uphill in parkland and finally broad flower basins of Adams Creek, its headwaters' branches flowing through Adams Creek Meadows.

The one flaw of High Camp (other than the punishment it takes in storms, evidenced by the streamlined clumps of trees) is that on any fine summer weekend it's a mob scene. But there's no need to put up with crowding. Throughout the vast meadowlands of Adams Creek Meadows on one side of the spur and Killen Meadows on the other are innumerable private nooks. Be careful of the fragile soil and camp only in established sites.

Old road:	123	101
New road:	23	2329

62 MADCAT MEADOW

Round trip 9 miles
Hiking time 4½ hours
High point 5800 feet
Elevation gain 1400 feet

Hikable July through October
One day or backpack
USGS Mt. Adams West

The meadows are very nice, if small, though perhaps not as interesting as their name. However, the close-up views of Avalanche and White Salmon Glaciers on the southwest side of Adams, and the views over the forested hinterland, abundantly reward the energy expenditure. Moreover, this is an excellent quick access to explorations high in the moraines.

Drive from Trout Lake on the road signed "Randle," in 1.2 miles turn left on road No. 23 ("Randle"), and at 8.8 miles from Trout Lake turn right on road No. 8031. In .4 mile from road No. 23 go left on road (8031)070, pass unsigned sideroads, and beware of deep, axle-busting waterbars. At 3.1 miles from road No. 23 go right on road (8031070)120 and at 3.9 miles find Stagman Ridge trail No. 12, elevation 4400 feet.

The trail begins in a clearcut, enters virgin forests of Mt. Adams Wilderness, and for some 1½ miles follows the long, gentle, wooded crest of Stagman Ridge, rounded on the west side, on the east an 800–1000-foot cliff to Cascade Creek. The way leaves the ridge and at about 3 miles forks. Stagman Ridge trail goes left ¾ mile to the Pacific Crest Trail. Keep straight ahead a few feet to Graveyard Camp, 5700 feet. Drop a bit and contour east, still in timber with occasional windows on Adams. At 4 miles from the road is little Looking Glass Lake, with campsite. Note that on the return the trail here easily can be missed.

The trail climbs another 200 feet to Meadow Camp, 4½ miles, 5800 feet. Countour east several hundred feet to Madcat Meadow and views south over green (moth-eaten) miles of Gifford Pinchot National Forest. Hidden in the trees are remains of a fire patrol storage shed dating from the early 1930s.

Follow the trail ½ mile more to the Round-the-Mountain trail and turn

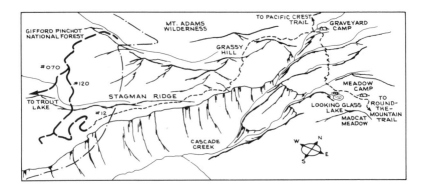

Madcat Meadow and Mount Rainier

east to unobstructed views of the glaciers; a basecamp hereabouts would give time for wandering to the uppermost meadows and to moraine crests so high as to be veritable mountains in their own right. Return the way you came or by walking west to the Pacific Crest Trail, thence to Stagman Ridge trail, and so home.

Old road:	123	N84	N840	N840	N840
New road:	23	23	8031	(8031)070	(8031070)120

63 MOUNT ADAMS HIGHLINE

One-way trip from Cold Springs
  Camp to Avalanche Valley 27½
  miles
Allow 3–4 days
High point 7760 feet
Elevation gain approximately
  4000 feet
Hikable mid-July through
  September
USGS Mt. Adams West, Mt. Adams
  East, Green Mountain, Glaciate
  Butte

Round trip from Killen Creek
  road to Avalanche Valley 26
  miles
Allow 3–4 days
High point 7760 feet
Elevation gain 4200 feet

The 34-mile timberline circuit of Mt. Adams is one of the greatest highland walks in the Cascades. Foregrounds of parkland and flowers

Camping near Foggy Bottom, Mount Rainier in distance

and waterfalls rise to lava jumbles that look like yesterday's eruptions to a succession of glaciers tumbling from the 12,326-foot summit. By day the hikers look out to miles of forested ridges and three other massive volcanoes. By night they gaze to megalopolitan skyglows of Puget Sound City, Yakima, and Portland.

However, you can't hardly do it. The Great Gap, the 4½ miles between Avalanche Valley and Bird Creek Meadows, has a half-dozen major glacial torrents to cross; one, the main branch of the the Big Muddy, often requires a dangerous bypass high on the Klickitat Glacier. There never has been and never can be a trail—not without huge expenditures and a miles-long detour down the valley to where bridges could be built (and annually rebuilt).

Moreover, 8 miles of the circuit—including the Gap—lie in the Yakima Indian Reservation and require obtaining a permit from the Yakima Indian Tribal Council in Toppenish, a process as complicated as the Big Muddy. For reasons of safety and politics we advise starting the journey not at Bird Creek Meadows, in the reservation, but at Cold Springs Campground.

From Highway 141 at Trout Lake drive north on road No. FH17, signed "Mt.Adams Recreation Area." Follow signs to Morrison Creek Campground and the end of road No. 8040 at Cold Springs, now called Timberline Campground, elevation 5600 feet. Hike 1 mile up abandoned road, now called trail No. 183, to the old Timberline Campground (often with no water) and at 6200 feet intersect the Mt. Adams Highline (or Round-the-Mountain) Trail No. 9.

To the right the trail contours 2 miles to the reservation boundary and legendary Bird Creek Meadows; the Yakimas allow day use here for $3 a day. An off-trail, meadow-contouring mile leads to a viewpoint at 6512 feet, an overlook of Hellroaring valley, this end of the Great Gap.

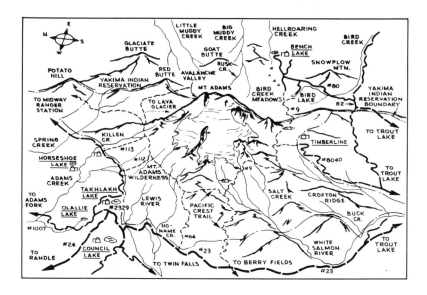

Avalanche Valley in the Yakima Indian Reservation

To the left the trail goes upsy-downsy, mainly in subalpine forest but with many meadow interludes and many vistas and many tempting sidetrips up to moraines and glaciers. Creeks and camps are frequent, though some of the glacial torrents are muddy, requiring the water to be settled in a pot to become palatable; a little milk never hurt anyone and adds body to the drink. At 6½ miles from the old Timberline Camp the Pacific Crest Trail is joined at Horseshoe Meadow, 5900 feet; a promontory just beyond gives a four-volcano vista, including the trip's last look at Hood.

Sidetrips continue to beckon as the Crest Trail proceeds north below little Crystal Lake and above little Sheep Lake, across the awesome Mutton Creek lava flow. At 14½ miles, 6100 feet, is the headwater creek of Lewis River; for a supreme basecamp, amble up the slope to meadowlands and settle down for days of exploring country below Pinnacle and Adams Glaciers. At 17 miles, 6084 feet, is a junction with Killen Creek trail No. 113 (Hike 61), 3 miles from the road; for hikers wishing to focus on Avalanche Valley this is the proper approach.

At 18 miles Killen Creek is crossed (camping) and in ¼ mile more Highline Trail No. 114 departs to the right from the Crest Trail, at 20½ miles entering the green of Foggy Flat, 6000 feet, a lovely meadow traversed by a clear brook. Now a stern uphill commences, from forest to the lava chaos below Lava Glacier—whose meltwater torrents may be impossible to cross—and at last tops out in the vast tundra barrens of Devils Gardens, 7760 feet. What a spot! Above are icefalls of Lyman and Wilson Glaciers, below is the volcanic vent of Red Butte. The winds they

Mount Adams from near Foggy Bottom

do howl up here, and the clouds do roll—though giant cairns mark the route, to attempt this saddle in a storm is to court hypothermia. Here, too, the reservation is entered.

The way drops to fine campsites in meadows of the Little Muddy, 7000 feet, 24½ miles, contours to a saddle between Mt. Adams and another volcanic vent, Goat Butte, and drops to Avalanche Valley, 6600 feet, 26½ miles, and trail's end. What's to say about this green vale where cold springs gush from lava tubes and meander through the flowers beneath cold walls of Wilson and Rusk Glaciers, beetling crags of Battlement Ridge, Victory Ridge, The Spearhead, The Castle, Roosevelt Cliff? Well, when good little hikers finally check in their boots, this is where they go.

Bad little hikers spend eternity in the 4½ miles of The Gap, staggering from moraine boulder to boulder, leaping Big Muddy and Hellroaring, trying to find the one and only semi-easy way over the Ridge of Wonders, never quite attaining Bird Creek Meadows at 34 miles to complete the circuit.

| Old road: | FH 17 | N700 | N80 | N81 |
| New road: | FH 17 | 82 | 80 | 8051 |

64 INDIAN HEAVEN LOOP

Short loop trip 10 miles
Hiking time 6 hours
High point 5237 feet
Elevation gain 1700 feet

Hikable July through October
One day or backpack
USGS Lone Butte and Wind River

A fascinating portion of the Pacific Crest Trail, with 17 lakes big enough to have names, 6 more on a short sidetrail, and almost 100 smaller lakes, ponds, and tadpole pools, all in an area of around 5000 feet elevation, a mixture of forest, groves of alpine trees, and flat, grassy meadows, the foregrounds complemented by occasional glimpses of glaciered volcanoes.

The region can be sampled by taking a one-day, 10-mile loop hike (described here), an overnight 18-mile loop, or by spending several days in order to include a visit to the Indian Racetrack, where the rut made by racing horses still indents a meadow used for centuries as a gathering place. The lakes usually melt free of snow early in July, but since Indian Heaven has been appropriately called "Mosquito Heaven," the trip is recommended for late August or September when the bugs are gone and, incidentally, the blueberries are ripe.

The starting point is Cultus Creek Campground, elevation 3988 feet, reached from Trout Lake on road No. 24. Follow signs to the Berry Fields. The campground is 3 miles south of the Berry Fields on road No. 24. The trailhead is in the back of a camp with no provision for cars, so park near the campground entrance in a lot reserved for hikers.

Whatever the chosen trip, start on trail No. 33, thus avoiding a very steep and hot ascent of 1200 feet on trail No. 108, which is better used for the return leg of the loop.

Trail No. 33 begins in forest, climbing 600 feet in the first mile. At 1¾ miles make the short sidetrip on trail 33A to Deep Lake with a view of Mt. Adams rising over treetops, then on to Cultus Lake at 2 miles, 5050 feet, a body of water typical of many of the lakes, having trees around half the shore, meadows around the rest. To the southeast is 5925-foot

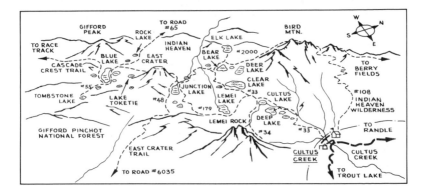

156

Small lake in Indian Heaven

Lemei Rock, and to the northwest, 5706-foot Bird Mountain; one or the other of these peaks can be seen from a number of the lakes. The way climbs 100 more feet, then descends to meet Lemei Lake trail No. 179. Keep right, staying on trail No. 33; pass within a few yards of Clear Lake, coming to Bear Lake at 4 miles. Cross the outlet (no problem) to join the Crest Trail on the far side, the return route for the longer loop. Head north on the Crest Trail, passing Deer Lake and numerous ponds. At about 7½ miles turn right on trail No. 108, climb over a 5237-foot saddle in Bird Mountain (a great view of Mt. Rainier), and drop steeply 1½ miles to Cultus Creek Campground.

Don't be fooled by the seemingly flat terrain—the paths have many short ups and downs. Campsites are numerous, some by lakes and others by streams. The pumice soil is very fragile, so camp in the forest or in already established campsites. The lakes and streams have a very small flow of water so to avoid contamination keep camps far away from the water's edge.

The Forest Service plans to reconstruct trail No. 33. The loop option will continue, but trailside scenery will change.

Old road: 123
New road: 24

Lake Wapiki

65 LAKE WAPIKI

Round trip 8½ miles
Hiking time 6 hours
High point 5685 feet
Elevation gain 1700 feet in, 500
  feet out

Hikable late July through
  October
One day or backpack
USGS Lone Butte and Sleeping
  Beauty

Every hiker of Indian Heaven has a favorite trip. Some like to immerse in bushels of lakes, as in Hike 64. Others home in on a single choice spot, such as Placid Lake or Junction Lake. But all connoisseurs agree Lake Wapiki, walled by cliffs on three sides, 5925-foot Lemei Rock towering above, is outstanding. The route described here throws in high viewpoints and wildflowers; the hiker not interested in these can use a shorter access from road No. 24.

Drive to Cultus Creek Campground (Hike 64) and park near the entrance in the area reserved for hikers' cars, elevation 3988 feet.

Begin on trail No. 33, climbing 1000 feet in 2 miles—steeply in spots—to Cultus Lake, 5100 feet. Round the shores and go left on trail No. 34, through heather, avalanche lilies, blueberries, with views of Adams and Rainier, the way climbing below the cliffs of Lemei Rock to just 250 feet of the summit, and a promontory 500 feet above Lake Wapiki. To aforementioned views add Hood, beyond the Columbia River, miles and miles of forest, and, in the distance, farm fields.

The trail descends ½ mile to a junction 4 miles from Cultus Creek Campground. Go right, gaining 100 feet in ¼ mile to the lake, a great place to camp—but be aware that some hikers also think it's a great place to swim.

Old road: 123
New road: 24

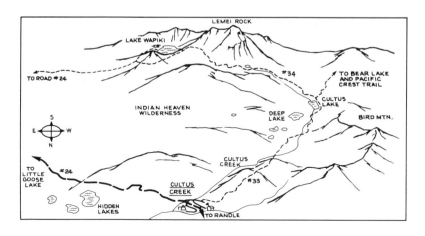

66   RACETRACK

Round trip 7 miles
Hiking time 4 hours
High point 4400 feet
Elevation gain 800 feet

Hikable mid-July through
  September
One day
USGS Wind River

In 1853 naturalist George Gibbs wrote (as quoted by Harry M. Majors in *Exploring Washington*), "The racing season is the grand annual occasion of these tribes. A horse of proved reputation is a source of wealth or of ruin to his owner. On his steed he stakes his whole stud, his household goods, clothes, and finally his wives. . . . They ride with skill, reckless of all obstacles, and with little mercy to their beasts, the right hand swinging the whip at every bound. . . . The Indians ride with hair-rope knotted around under their jaw for a bridle. The men use a stuffed pad, with wooden stirrups."

The Klickitat and Yakima peoples came here in late summer to pick huckleberries and dry them in the sun. The highland then was a vast berry field, possibly because the harvesters regularly set fires to burn encroaching forests, or because the Little Ice Age had kept the treeline at lower elevations, or a combination.

For centuries, maybe eons, they traveled perhaps the trails we now walk, to places suitable for combining the berry harvest with picniclike socializing. Having at some time in the 18th century acquired horses from neighbors (ultimately from the Spanish in Mexico), they began to bring them for the sport Gibbs observed. In the Racetrack meadow they wore a rut 2000 feet long, but only a few hundred feet can be seen, trees having invaded most of the meadow; despite modern horse riders who like to run their mounts along it, the rut is mere inches deep. This isn't a place to see history. But if you sit a spell picking huckleberries you can feel it.

From Trout Lake drive to the Berry Fields, then south on Wind River

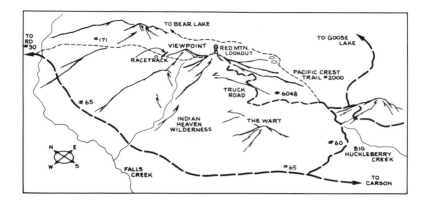

Racetrack and Mount St. Helens

road No. 30 for some 7 miles. Go left 6.6 miles on road No. 65 to Racetrack trail No. 171, elevation 3500 feet. (From the south drive north from Carson 10 miles on Wind River highway, go right 10.6 miles on road No. 60, signed "Carson-Guler," and turn left 5 miles on road No. 65 to the trailhead.)

In ¼ mile the trail reaches Falls Creek, the only all-summer water on this route, and in early summer it's too much water, the boulder-hop crossing not rationally possible. However, since the huckleberry time of September is the usual time of a hike (unless one wishes to see the acres of beargrass blooming in mid-July), the creek generally is more pleasing than repelling. For 1 mile the trail climbs rather briskly, then levels off and drops a bit to the Racetrack, 2½ miles, 4300 feet, near a pond that dries up in summer.

For the best overview of the Racetrack meadow, climb the steep Red Mountain trail in woods to the top of the first hill, leave the trail, and ascend north on pumice slopes to a bare knoll with an aerial 4700-foot perspective 3½ miles from road No. 65. (The car-accessible views from Red Mountain Lookout to the horizon are very fine, but that's not wilderness, and moreover the Racetrack can't be seen from there.)

| Old road: | N605 | N60 |
| New road: | 65 | 60 |

67 OBSERVATION (TRAPPER) PEAK LOOP

Round trip from Government Mineral Springs 12 miles
Hiking time 7½ hours
High point 4207 feet
Elevation gain 2900 feet
Hikable June through September
One day
USGS Lookout Mountain, Wind River

Round trip from road No. 58 6 miles
Hiking time 3 hours
Elevation gain 1600 feet in, 300 feet out

A loop trip through forest from the valley bottom to the 4207-foot summit of Observation Peak, site of the old Trapper Lookout, with a panoramic view of the Wind River valley, or an easier ridge walk with meadows and vistas.

For the loop trip drive Wind River highway 15 miles north from Carson to Government Mineral Springs. Cross the Wind River and in .25 mile turn right on road No. 5401; drive a short distance farther to where the road is gated, and find the trailhead, elevation 1300 feet.

Observation Peak trail No. 132 parallels a summer-home road 1 mile to a junction with the Trapper Creek trail. From there the peak trail climbs steeply up the south side of Howe Ridge with fleeting views through trees. At 3 miles cross a small stream which may be the last water. At 4½ miles the way swings around the north side of the ridge. At 6½ miles is a junction with Ridge trail No. 157 (see below). Keep climbing a final ½ mile to the peak and views, views, and more views. For the return go back to the junction with No. 157, follow it west ½ mile, then descend Big Hollow trail No. 158, which runs into Dry Creek trail No. 194, ending at the same trailhead you started from.

For the Ridge Trail drive Wind River road to within ½ mile of Government Mineral Springs, just short of Wind River bridge. Keep right on road No. 30. At 2 miles turn left on Dry Creek road No. 64 for 8 miles,

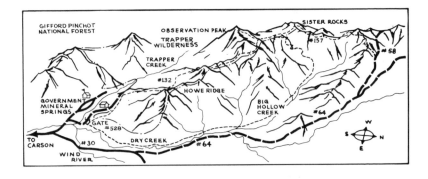

Trapper Peak and Mount Hood

then go left on road No. 58 for 2 more miles and find the trailhead on the east side of the road, elevation 3200 feet.

Ridge trail No. 157 sets out in virgin forest of Sister Rocks Research Natural Area, gaining 800 feet. Then, at about 1 mile, it enters an old burn grown up in huckleberries and flowers and drops 300 feet along the ridge connecting Sister Rocks to Observation (Trapper) Peak. At 1¾ miles is Observation Camp (water is sometimes to be found in a spring on the north side of the ridge). At 2½ miles is the junction with the trail from Government Mineral Springs.

For an interesting sidetrip wander up meadows of flowers and huckleberries to the top of Sister Rocks, 4261 feet. Near the top are traces of an old trail, a few telephone poles, and bits of melted glass, all the remains of Sister Rocks Lookout.

Old road:	N73	N64	N63
New road:	30	64	58

68 SIOUXON CREEK

Round trip 10 miles
Hiking time 5 hours
High point 1900 feet
Elevation gain 1000 feet in, 600
feet out

Hikable March through
November
One day or backpack
USGS Lookout Mountain

The canopy is interwoven branches of tall firs, hemlocks, and maples.
The floor is moss, oxalis, and ferns. Beside the path ripples and tumbles
Siouxon Creek, a lowland stream whose limeade pools invite a person to
mingle with the fish. Joyous camps are plentiful and, should a person feel
energetic, the summit of 4108-foot Huffman Peak is there for views of St.
Helens and plenty more. But hurry (to hike, and to write your con-
gressperson): the logging roads are in and the chainsaws are tuning up,
for Siouxon Creek was excluded from the 1984 Washington Wilderness
Act.

Drive from the headquarters of Mt. St. Helens National Monument in
Chelatche (4 miles from Amboy and 12 miles from Cougar) north on
Canyon Creek road, past a sawmill and farms. At 1.3 miles cross a private logging road and the start of road No. 24. At 9 miles from Chelatche
turn left on road No. 57, climbing steeply. At 10.3 miles turn left again
on road No. 5701. At 11 miles the road switchbacks, intersecting the
one-time beginning of the trail. Continue onward and at 13 miles (from
Chelatche) reach the (1985) end of the road and the trailhead, elevation
1550 feet.

A spur path drops a hundred feet into forest to join Siouxon Creek trail
No. 130, which plummets 300 feet more to the banks of Siouxon Creek
and a crossing of West Creek on logs. The way wends upstream on the
valley floor, campsites inviting frequently.

In 1 mile pass Horseshoe Ridge trail No. 140, which climbs to a logging

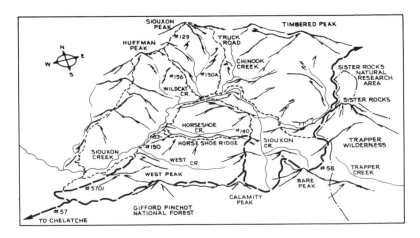

Siouxon Creek

road and a 3495-foot promontory, former site of Horseshoe Ridge Lookout. At about 1½ miles the trail crosses Horseshoe Creek and climbs 400 feet over a cliff and drops back to the creek, a good bit of exercise. At 2½ miles is an intersection with trail No. 156 (see below) and in a bit more a crossing of Siouxon Creek on a log to a junction with trail No. 130A, which climbs to logging roads on Siouxon Peak. (There is no safety here without Wilderness; the trees are falling on every side.) Keep right along Siouxon Creek, crossing Chinook Creek at 3 miles, and at 5 miles, 1900 feet, Siouxon Creek again. This is a good turnaround; from here the trail climbs from the valley to road No. 58, near Sister Rocks.

The promised scenic sidetrip: At 2½ miles take trail No. 156 (see above) up Wildcat Ridge to Siouxon Ridge, then go west on trail No. 129 in trees, meadows, and rocky slopes to 4106-foot Huffman Peak, a former lookout site. The sidetrip is 3½ miles each way and gains 2700 feet, a lot.

There is no bridge at either end of this sidetrip, so plan on doing this trail in late summer when the water is low.

For a loop: From Huffman Peak walk 5 miles down the ridge to Siouxon Creek and 2 more miles back to the start.

Old road:	N56	N54	N54A
New road:	24	57	5701

69 DOG MOUNTAIN

Round trip 7 miles
Hiking time 5 hours
High point 3100 feet
Elevation gain 3000 feet

Hikable April through October
One day
USGS Hood River

The Columbia Gorge, where the downcutting by the legendary River of the West has kept pace with the uprising of the Cascade Range across its path—the river literally older than the mountain—is a national scenic treasure if ever there was one. Yet developers demand their "rights" and most politicians are eager to "compromise" the game away. A hiker can go far toward judging the relative merits of positions by walking a former stretch of the Cascade Crest Trail to a former lookout with views across the gorge to Mt. Hood, and up and down the river.

Drive Highway 14 on the Washington side of the Columbia 9 miles east from Stevenson to a large (probably unmarked) parking area for Dog Mountain trail No. 147, elevation 186 feet.

The trail gains some 700 feet in forest (watch for snakes and poison oak, both beautiful in their own ways but best enjoyed at a distance), joins an excruciatingly steep logging road unlikely ever to have been negotiated by any ordinary truck, and at about 1200 feet returns to trail.

A lengthy zigzagging leads out of forest to the prairie-subalpine spring blooming of buttercups and asters, lupine and paintbrush, and scores of other flowers. At 2½ miles, 2400 feet, is the site of Puppy Lookout, so called because it was only partway up Dog Mountain. The cabin was on a shelf dug from the hillside. Here are the best river views; only the tip of Hood can be seen.

For more wildflowers as the season progresses, and bigger views of Hood, continue another mile to the top of Dog Mountain, 3100 feet, 3½ miles. Do you have any remaining doubts about the worthiness of preserving the Columbia Gorge for the nation?

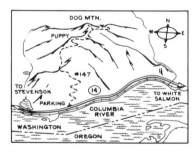

Columbia River from Dog Mountain trail

Pacific Crest Trail near Snowgrass Flat, Mount Adams in distance

70   PACIFIC CREST TRAIL

The Pacific Crest National Scenic Trail, which extends from Mexico to Canada, is most commonly called in the northernmost 500 miles by its older name, the Cascade Crest Trail. The 246-mile portion between the Columbia River and Snoqualmie Pass traverses highlands past three grand volcanoes and through the spectacular ruins of a fourth. The way isn't all pure fun because it also goes through lower, forested sections of the Cascade Range where logging roads and clearcuts have savaged the wilderness solitude. However, the feeling of accomplishment gained by traveling the full length of the crest cannot be spoiled even by the worst of the messed-up parts.

Few hikers complete the route in a single effort; most do the trail in short bits over a period of years. Those taking the whole trip at once can start at either end; the south-to-north direction is described here.

At many places the trail is being relocated for the sake of easier grades or better scenery. The following brief summary is intended merely to provide a general impression of the route. For details of mileages and campsites, consult the Forest Service map and log of the Pacific Crest Trail, available from any Forest Service office.

COLUMBIA RIVER TO WHITE PASS

One-way trip about 148 miles
Hiking time 15 days minimum
High point 7620 feet
Elevation gain about 24,900 feet
Hikable May the first 27 miles,
   mid-July the rest

USGS Hood River, Wind River,
   Willard, Steamboat Mountain,
   Mt. Adams West, Green
   Mountain, Walupt Lake, White
   Pass

Begin beside the River of the West, skirt the slopes of giant Mt. Adams, enjoy views to what's left of graceful Mt. St. Helens, and walk the airy crest of the Goat Rocks Wilderness—the most difficult, as well as one of the most dramatically beautiful, segments of the entire Crest Trail.

Drive Highway 14 east from Vancouver to the Bridge of the Gods and locate the trailhead parking lot on the north side of the highway, elevation 186 feet.

Hike through forest and lava flows with occasional views. The route is interrupted by logging roads, clearcuts, powerlines, and pipelines. Go up and down several times. Unless it is coming from the sky, there is no water for the first 12 miles. The trail crosses Wind River and, shortly after, road No. 30. The way climbs to Big Mountain and then drops to road No. 60 and a dry camp. **Distance from the Columbia River to road No. 60 about 45 miles; elevation gain 7900 feet; hiking time 5 days.**

From road No. 60 climb miles of woods to Red Mountain and Blue Lake and the pond-dotted meadows and famous huckleberry fields of Indian Heaven (Hike 64). Pass near Bear Lake, go almost over the top of Sawtooth Mountain, cross road No. 24, and continue through Huckleberry Meadows to Mosquito Creek. Cross the road again and traverse the east side of Steamboat Mountain to a third crossing of road No. 24. **Distance from road No. 60 to road No. 24 about 26 miles; elevation gain about 2900 feet; hiking time 3 days.**

The next stage is climaxed by the alpine gardens and glacial streams on the flanks of Mt. Adams. From road No. 24 cross road No. 88, Trout Lake Creek, and road No. 8810, climb to Dry Meadows and Grand Meadows, cross road No. 23, traverse Swampy Meadows, and at 12 miles join the Mt. Adams Highline Trail (Hike 63). At 22 miles leave the Highline Trail and at 23½ miles leave the Mt. Adams Wilderness at Spring Creek and proceed to road No. 2329 at Midway Meadows. **Distance from road No. 24 to Midway Meadows about 29 miles; elevation gain about 3500 feet; hiking time 3 days.**

Now starts the first long stretch of roadless country, most of it in the

Goat Rocks Wilderness, including a couple of miles that can be dangerous. From Midway Meadows go a short bit along a rough road, round a lava flow, and at 6 miles enter the Wilderness. Proceed past Coleman Weedpatch, intersect the Walupt Lake trail, and pass above Snowgrass Flat (Hike 44). Carefully, bewaring of hazards, climb the ridge above Packwood Glacier and traverse the shoulder of Old Snowy to Elk Pass (Hike 45). The route crosses above to McCall Basin, Tieton Pass, and Shoe Lake (Hike 39), at 34 miles leaving the Wilderness and descending to White Pass. **Distance from Midway Meadows to White Pass about 38 miles; elevation gain about 6100 feet; hiking time 4 to 5 days.**

WHITE PASS TO SNOQUALMIE PASS

One-way trip about 98 miles
Hiking time 13 days
High point 6500 feet

Elevation gain about 20,400 feet
Hikable mid-July through October
USGS White Pass, Bumping Lake, Lester, Snoqualmie Pass

North from White Pass extend miles of marvelous meadows and lakes and large views of Mt. Rainier in the William O. Douglas and Norse Peak Wildernesses, then a lower and more wooded (and road-marred) section of the crest leading to Snoqualmie Pass.

The first stage rarely leaves meadows and panoramas for long and passes numerous small lakes—too many to name here. From the White Pass highway hike to Sand Lake (Hike 29), Cowlitz Pass, Fish Lake, and the Mt. Rainier National Park boundary at 15½ miles. Weave in and out of the park, following the crest by Two Lakes, Dewey Lakes, and around the side of Naches Peak to Chinook Pass and US 410; here leave the national park. **Distance from White Pass to Chinook Pass about 25 miles; elevation gain about 2400 feet; hiking time 3 days.**

The opening third of the next part lies in alpine terrain as before, and the remainder in woods broken by roads. Climb from Chinook Pass to Sourdough Gap (Hike 13), traverse to Bear Gap and around Pickhandle Point and Crown Point, with views to the Crystal Mountain Ski Area, ascend the crest, contour below the summit of Norse Peak, and drop into Big Crow Basin. Proceed to Little Crow Basin, a junction with the Arch Rock trail, Arch Rock Camp, and Rod's Gap. Pass Government Meadows and cross the Naches Wagon Trail (Hike 8); contour under Pyramid Peak to Windy Gap. **Distance from Chinook Pass to Windy Gap about 27 miles; elevation gain about 2500 feet; hiking time 3 days.**

Now comes a portion with few views except in clearcuts. From Windy Gap follow the crest nearly to the top of Blowout Mountain, descend in woods and clearcuts to Tacoma Pass and a logging road, and travel onward under Snowshoe Butte to Lizard Lake and the road at Stampede Pass. **Distance from Windy Gap to Stampede Pass about 27 miles; elevation gain about 1100 feet; hiking time 3 days.**

More forest travel—but much of the private land is being logged so the path is not always easy to find and not always pleasant, despite increasingly mountainous views northward. From Stampede Pass hike to Dandy Pass and Mirror Lake, contour Tinkham and Silver Peaks (Hike 3) to Olallie Meadow and Lodge Lake, climb to Beaver Lake, and drop down ski slopes to Snoqualmie Pass. **Distance from Stampede Pass to Snoqualmie Pass about 18 miles; elevation gain about 1400 feet; hiking time 2 days.**

From Snoqualmie Pass the Pacific Crest Trail continues 253 miles to Allison Pass in Canada. See *100 Hikes in the Alpine Lakes* and *100 Hikes in the North Cascades.*

| Old road: | N60 | 123 | N88 | 101 |
| New road: | 60 | 24 | 88 | 2324 |

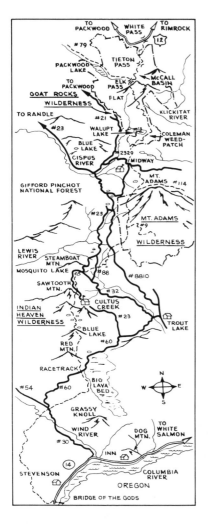

71 SUNDOWN PASS

Round trip about 15 miles
Hiking time 10 hours
High point 4103 feet
Elevation gain 2800 feet in, 300 feet out

Hikable late July through October
One day or backpack
USGS Mt. Steel and Mt. Christie

Good trail follows a loud river through big-tree forest, then poor trail ascends to heather meadows and a delightful lakelet. The lower valley invites day hikes and riverbank camps tempt a person to lounge overnight, listening to the water, looking at the trees—and trying to understand why the South Fork Skokomish River was omitted from the Wonder Mountain Wilderness established in 1984.

Drive US 101 between Shelton and Hoodsport to .6 mile south of the Skokomish River bridge, turn upvalley on the Skokomish River road 5.5 miles, and go right on road No. 23. Stick with it through many surprising twists and turns, taking care to dodge sideroads to Browns Creek Campground, Spider Lake, and Pine Lake. At 19 miles from the highway go left on road No. 2319, pass two trailheads to Lower South Fork Skokomish River trail, and at 24.5 miles come to the end of the road and the start of Upper South Fork Skokomish River trail No. 873, elevation 1300 feet.

Sundown Lake

The beginning is in deep forest interspersed with huge boulders that in the dim past were thousands of feet above, part of the mountain. At ½ mile cross Rule Creek and the South Fork on logs; by now, observing the beautiful large trees, you see why they were not given protection by the Washington Wilderness Act of 1984 and why they are on our agenda for Wilderness Act II. At 2 miles recross the river on a log. At a very long 3 miles a log spans Startup Creek to the last riverside camp. The trail starts up, for sure, then contours steep slopes to the boundary of Olympic National Park, about 4½ miles, 2800 feet. The good news is that here begins wilderness protection. What not everyone will consider even better news is that the wilderness is guarded not only by statute but by the end of good trail; the way trail beyond here receives little maintenance, is easy to lose, and shouldn't be attempted until all the snow melts, revealing boot-beaten tread, a help in route finding.

Sometimes ascending ladderways of roots, other times traversing, the way is marked by metal tabs on trees and plastic ribbon. About ½ mile into the park is Camp Riley, in soggy meadows trampled by a herd of elk, many of whose trails are better than the official one; cross the greenery and search for plastic ribbons; if you go more than a few hundred feet with no definite sign of humanity, return to the last ribbon and try again.

Beyond the meadows the trail climbs steeply, then levels out in a nice subalpine meadow. The trail appears to be intent on crossing the meadow but in fact only skirts it a short bit before turning right, back into the woods; be wary, watch for ribbons. The trail tilts up and traverses to the right, ascending heather meadows dotted by small tarns. Above the highest, look for ribbons and ascend to Sundown Pass, 4103 feet, approximately 6½ miles from the road.

Good tread descends 300 feet in ½ mile to a junction with Graves Creek trail and in a level ½ mile reaches Sundown Lake, 7½ miles.

| Old road: | 226 | 239 | 239 |
| New road: | 23 | 23 | 2319 |

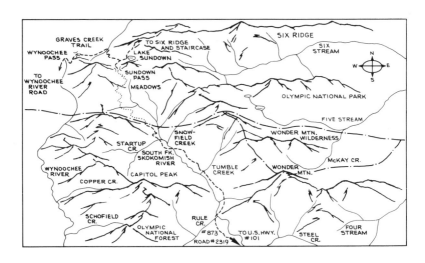

72 MOUNT ELLINOR

Round trip to timberline 2½ miles
Hiking time 2 hours
High point 4500 feet
Elevation gain 1000 feet

Hikable July through October
One day
USGS Mt. Steele and The Brothers

From 1853 to 1857 George Davidson surveyed Puget Sound, working from the brig *R. H. Fauntleroy,* named for his superior, the head of the U.S. Coast and Geodetic Survey. Needing names for the maps he was making, he drew upon the Fauntleroy family, calling the southernmost prominent peak on the Olympic skyline Ellinor, for the youngest daughter, the double-summited peak for her Brothers, and the highest point for her older sister Constance. Later, Davidson and Ellinor were married. However, subsequent mappers shifted Ellinor to a lower peak, replacing her with Mt. Washington.

A century and more later, hikers look from Ellinor over a panorama of the Cascades from Mt. St. Helens to Glacier Peak, and of the Olympics from neighboring Mt. Washington, whose profile can be imagined to resemble that of the general and president, to the distant white mass of Mt. Olympus.

Drive US 101 along Hood Canal to Hoodsport. Turn west 9 miles on the Lake Cushman road to a junction. Turn right 1.6 miles on road No. 24, then left 4.9 miles on Big Creek road No. 2419 to the signed trailhead. Though the trail will be kept open from this start, for a shorter hike continue on the road to the first Y, take the left fork to the end, and there find an unsigned trailhead, elevation about 3500 feet. Carry a full canteen; the slopes are dry.

Find a boot-built path climbing to the ridge top. At 1¼ miles, about

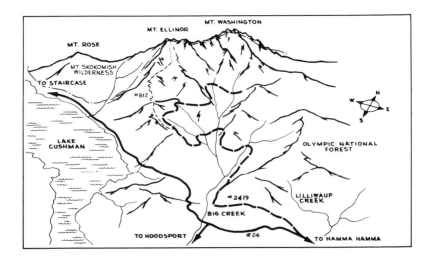

Hood Canal and Mount Rainier from trail's end on Mount Ellinor

4500 feet, is timberline and the trail-end, and for inexperienced hikers, the proper turnaround. The vistas of lowlands and Cascades are as good here as from the 5944-foot summit—and there is no danger of getting lost, as there may be on the final slopes.

The temptation to go on is overwhelming; to the inexperienced eye, the gully from trail-end to summit looks simple. It's not. The gully is steeper than it appears and the rocks are sometimes slippery and always loose—terrain for an experienced rock scrambler. Should the fog roll in, one easily can stray into the wrong gully and get lost. If a person wants to go for the top of the mountain, he should choose a quiet weekday rather than a mobbed weekend, or come in early summer when the road is still snowbound.

Old road: 245   2419
New road: 24   2419

73 FLAPJACK LAKES

Round trip to lakes 15.6 miles	**One day or backpack**
Hiking time 10 hours	**USGS Mt. Steel**
High point 4000 feet	**Park Service backcountry use**
Elevation gain 3100 feet	**permit required**
Hikable July through October	

Two subalpine lakes set side by side like flapjacks in a frying pan. Above the waters and the forests rise sharp summits of the Sawtooth Range, a group of peaks noted among climbers for the odd texture of the rock, which largely consists of "pillow lava" erupted under the surface of an ancient sea and now eroded into weird shapes.

Drive US 101 along Hood Canal to Hoodsport. Turn west to Lake Cushman and follow the North Fork Skokomish River road to Staircase Ranger Station and the trailhead, elevation 800 feet.

The trail follows an abandoned road the first 3¾ miles, then ascends moderately but steadily in cool forest to a junction at 7¼ miles. From here a faint way trail goes left to Black and White Lakes in 1⅓ miles, Smith Lake in 2¼ miles.

The right fork reaches Flapjack Lakes, 4000 feet, in ½ mile. One lake, quite shallow, is well along toward becoming a marsh, while the other is deeper and ringed by rock buttresses; the two are separated by a narrow isthmus. The most striking Sawtooth summit from the lake is The Horn—known to a party of hikers, who saw it on an autumn night years ago with the full moon (made of green cheese, then) touching its yearning snout, as "The Mouse."

Actually, the trip only just begins at the lakes. For high and wide meadows and broad views, walk the Mt. Gladys way trail 1½ more miles up a lovely valley of rocks and flowers and bubbling water to Gladys Pass, 5000 feet, between a rounded garden peak and a vicious finger of

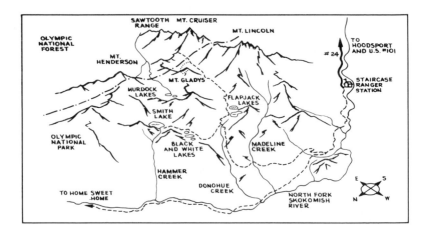

Upper Flapjack Lake and Mount Lincoln

lava. Roam the gardens to the 5600-foot summit of Mt. Gladys. Stare at the frightening walls of 6104-foot Cruiser ("Bruiser") Peak, whose tower is visible from Seattle, standing like a boundary monument on the southeast corner of Olympic National Park.

Popularity has forced stringent restrictions on camping: a nightly limit of 30 persons at the lakes and above; stoves only at the lakes and above (wood fires permitted below Donahue Creek). Alternative campsites are at Smith Lake and the scenic Black and White Lakes.

Mount Steel near Home Sweet Home, taken in late June

HOOD CANAL
Olympic National Park

74   HOME SWEET HOME

Round trip to Camp Pleasant 13 miles
Hiking time 8 hours
High point 1600 feet
Elevation gain 800 feet
Hikable May through November
One day or backpack
USGS Mt. Steel

Round trip to Home Sweet Home 26 miles
Allow 2 days
High point 5688 feet
Elevation gain 4000 feet in, 500 feet out
Hikable mid-July through October
Park Service backcountry use permit required

In early May, when a small elk herd is still in the Skokomish valley and trillium and calypso orchids are in bloom, walk the gentle trail to

Nine Stream. In summer, climb from the valley to First Divide and broad views, then drop to Duckabush River drainage and the lupine meadows of Home Sweet Home.

Drive US 101 to Hoodsport and turn west to the end of the North Fork Skokomish River road (Hike 73), elevation 800 feet.

The North Fork Skokomish River trail follows an abandoned road almost 3¾ miles, then enters forest to Big Log Camp, 5½ miles, a spacious area beside the stream. At 6 miles the way crosses the river on a bridge over a deep, quiet pool. Immediately beyond is a junction; go right. The trail climbs slightly to Camp Pleasant, 6½ miles, 1600 feet, on a large maple flat. This appropriately named spot makes a good overnight stop for springtime backpackers.

At 9½ miles, 2091 feet, is Nine Stream and the end of level walking. In the next mile the trail ascends at a comfortable rate through a big meadow, then forest. After that the way is continously steep and often rough. Flower gardens become more frequent. Mt. Sone appears to the south.

At about 12 miles the trail reaches a meadow below Mt. Steel, turns sharply right, and climbs to the crest of 4688-foot First Divide, 12½ miles, and views across the Duckabush valley to Mt. LaCrosse, White Mountain, and the greenery of LaCrosse Pass.

The path descends ½ mile to Home Sweet Home, 4198 feet, where one may enjoy the blossoms of avalanche lilies or lupine, depending on the season. The view is superb of 6233-foot Mt. Steel.

From First Divide a faint way trail goes around the south side of Mt. Hopper, but the route is rough and best left to very experienced travelers.

Many hikers continue from Home Sweet Home to Lake LaCrosse (Hike 96), 7 miles farther, with a loss of 2000 feet followed by a stiff gain of 2500 feet to the lake. From there they either proceed onward around O'Neil Pass to the Enchanted Valley trail or over Anderson Pass to the Dosewallips trail.

A few hikers drop from Home Sweet Home to the Duckabush River, hike 1½ miles downstream, and climb over 5566-foot LaCrosse Pass to Honeymoon Meadows on the Dosewallips (Hike 80). Only the vast meadows at the pass make this grueling 3000-foot ascent on a waterless, south-facing slop worth the effort.

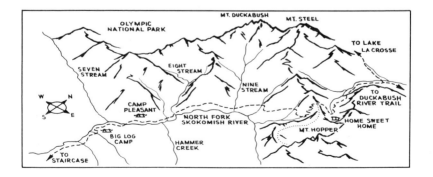

75 MILDRED LAKES

Round trip about 10 miles
Hiking time 8 hours
High point 4100 feet
Elevation gain 2300 feet in, 600
 feet out

Hikable mid-July through
 mid-October
Backpack
USGS Mt. Steel

Three mountain lakes beneath the startling basalt spires of Sawtooth Ridge, well worth a visit—as they'd darn well better be, after the struggle. The trail (way), not recognized by the Forest Service as part of its system, and on certain wooded slopes so obscure the hiker may not recognize it either, has been hammered into hillsides and over countless logs by generations of fishermen, hikers, and climbers. The distance is only 4 miles (or is it 5?), but that doesn't include detours around wooden barricades. Nor does the figure given here for elevation include the ups and downs over logs and rocks and bumps. These are just extra dividends. But don't complain—even more than the official designation by Congress in 1984, they make it *real* wilderness.

Drive 14 miles up Hamma Hamma road No. 25 (Hike 76) to the end at a concrete bridge over the Hamma Hamma River, elevation 1900 feet. Find the trail at the far side of the bridge and enter Mt. Skokomish Wilderness.

On the first mile a little work has been done—logs cut, the tread occasionally graded. Such gestures end in the second mile as the way climbs steeply over a 3200-foot ridge and drops 300 feet to a delightful camp beside a brook, approximately 2½ miles. The trail is easily lost here amid false paths made by mixed-up hikers.

Cross the creek, stay level several hundred feet, then climb—and climb, with only an occasional respite, 1000 feet, mostly straight up. At 4100 feet is a ridge top of heather and alpine trees and great views that tempt a party to call it quits. Don't. The madding crowd has been left behind. The end is near. Drop 300 feet to Lower Mildred Lake, follow the path along the shore to the lakehead, and near the inlet find the trail (again, amid many false paths) climbing a bit more than 300 feet in ⅓

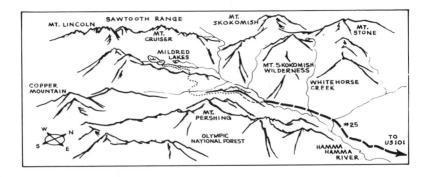

Upper Mildred Lake and Sawtooth Range

mile to the upper lake and great views and great camps.

The third lake, about the same elevation, is off toward Mt. Cruiser. The path starts from the outlet of the upper lake.

If time permits, ascend (with some bushwhacking) a 5000-foot knoll below Mt. Lincoln. The effort is repaid with a view of Mt. Washington, Mt. Pershing, and a score of other Olympic peaks.

Old road: 249
New road: 25

76   UPPER LENA LAKE

Round trip to upper lake 14 miles
Hiking time 12 hours
High point 4600 feet
Elevation gain 3900 feet
Hikable April through November
  to lower lake

Hikable July through October to
  upper lake
One day or backpack
USGS The Brothers
Park Service backcountry use
  permit required

Hike an easy trail, free of snow most of the year, through splendid forest to popular and often crowded Lower Lena Lake. The lake should have been part of The Brothers Wilderness but was left out because of a proposed hydroelectric project. This project would be so damaging to hikers, the Forest Service and environmental groups are protesting the proposal.

Drive US 101 along Hood Canal to Eldon. Turn west on the Hamma Hamma River road about 9 miles to Phantom Creek and .5 mile beyond to the trailhead, elevation 685 feet.

The wide trail switchbacks gently and endlessly in forest shadows. At about 1½ miles the way crosses the dry stream bed of Lena Creek which runs underground most of the year. At 3 miles reach Lower Lena Lake, 1800 feet. Here the trail splits.

The right fork drops to campsites by the lake and rounds the west shore ½ mile to more. At a junction turn right to follow East Fork Lena Creek into the Valley of Silent Men, crossing and recrossing the stream many times, toward The Brothers, a principal summit of the Olympic

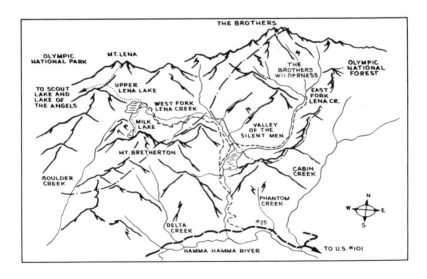

Upper Lena Lake and Mount Bretherton

horizon seen from Seattle. This ancient miner's trail into The Brothers Wilderness is mainly used by fishermen and climbers but is well worth exploration by hikers who enjoy loitering beside cold water frothing and sparkling through rapids, swirling in green pools, all in the deep shade of old forest.

The left fork follows West Fork Lena Creek, entering Olympic National Park at 4 miles. At approximately 5 miles, 2700 feet, the trail crosses a small creek and becomes steep and badly eroded. The present trail was built in the late 1930s. It was steep then, but the tread was smooth and wide. Subsequently a few windfalls have been cut but otherwise there has been no maintenance. Floods, slides, and fallen trees have taken their toll and only remnants of the original tread remain.

As the trail climbs, the vegetation changes to subalpine forest. Heather and huckleberry appear along with Alaska cedar. There are occasional views down the valley toward The Brothers. The steepness ends abruptly at Upper Lena Lake, 4600 feet, 7 miles. A rough up-and-down way trail rounds the north side.

Camps are inviting but have been overused and some are being revegetated by the Park Service; camp only at designated sites; no wood fires, stoves only. The shore demands roaming, as do the meadows and screes ringing the cirque. For more ambitious explorations scramble to the summit of 5998-foot Mt. Lena or ascend the boot-beaten path beside the small creek falling from little Milk Lake, tucked in a quiet pocket and generally frozen until late summer, or follow a track over a 5000-foot ridge near Mt. Lena to Scout Lake, or follow the ridge with its numerous tarns toward Mt. Stone and Lake of the Angels.

Duckabush River

HOOD CANAL
The Brothers Wilderness

77 DUCKABUSH RIVER

Round trip 10 miles
Hiking time 6 hours
High point 2100 feet
**Elevation gain 1700 feet in, 800
    feet out**

Hikable May through November
One day or backpack
USGS The Brothers

The Duckabush River trail is 20 miles long, wildland all the way to
Lake LaCrosse and O'Neil Pass (Hike 96) in the heart of the Olympics,
and the hiker who takes this respectful forest approach truly earns the

highland gardens. However, the lower stretch of trail, in forest of 200- to 400-year-old firs and hemlocks, with sumptuous riverside camps, is a trip on its own, particularly enjoyed in late spring and early summer when the snow is still deep on the heights but is gone here, replaced by the blooms of bead lily and calypso orchid. It's not all a garden path; there are two major obstacles, Little Hump and Big Hump, but for reasons to be explained, you shouldn't complain.

Drive US 101 to .2 mile north of the Duckabush River bridge and turn off on the Duckabush River road, which at 3.7 miles becomes road No. 2515. At 6 miles turn right on road No. (2515)011 and in .1 mile find Duckabush River trail No. 803, elevation 500 feet.

The trail gets directly to business, climbing the first obstacle on a long-abandoned road, gaining 400 feet in 1 mile to the top of Little Hump and the boundary of The Brothers Wilderness. Solitude is not assured from here on, but Little Hump weeds out the pikers among the hikers.

The way drops 200 feet (oh! oh!) to river level and for 1 mile of flat valley bottom follows an old logging railroad grade through half-century-old second growth from the 1920s and 1930s. At 2¼ miles is a good camp.

Excellent if steep trail now tackles the main job, Big Hump. While toiling up 1000 feet, reflect that it was the Big Hump that stopped the logging railroad in the 1930s, as well as the truck loggers of later decades, saving this forest—which you will notice is now virgin—for wilderness designation in 1984. So, no complaints. At 3½ miles a false summit gives views across the valley to St. Peters Dome and downstream, and at 3¾ miles the way tops Big Hump. And promptly drops 600 feet (no complaints!) to the river and a great campsite at 1100 feet, about 5 miles from the road.

A scant 1½ miles leads to the park boundary and more camps.

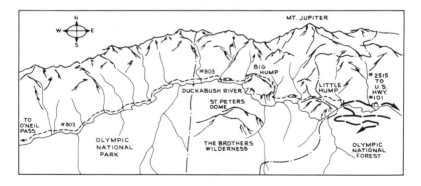

185

78 MOUNT JUPITER

Round trip 14 miles
Hiking time 10 hours
High point 5701 feet
Elevation gain 3600 feet

Hikable June through October
One day
USGS Point Misery and The
  Brothers

Look from Seattle across Puget Sound to the Olympic horizon; right smack between The Brothers and Mt. Constance is Jupiter. Actually, the peak does not deserve inclusion in such distinguished company, but stands so far out in the front of the range as to seem bigger than it really is. And in fact, old Jupe offers unique combination views of lowlands and mountains. The summit ascent, however, is long and strenuous and usually dry and hot. Most hikers are content to climb the trail to the views and leave the summit to peakbaggers. Carry a loaded canteen—there is no water on the way.

Drive US 101 along Hood Canal to a short mile north of the Duckabush River bridge. A bit south of the Black Point road, turn west 3.5 miles on unsigned Mt. Jupiter road No. 2620 to a junction. Turn left on the fork (sometimes) signed "Mt. Jupiter Trail" (and "2620-011") and drive 3 steep and tortuous miles to the trailhead, elevation 2150 feet. (*Note:* Due to recent logging on state and private land, the road route is hard to stay on.)

The first mile switchbacks up south slopes of the ridge dividing the Duckabush and Dosewallips Rivers. At 1 mile, 2850 feet, the trail reaches the ridge crest and here leaves state land and enters Olympic National Forest. The hike to this point, with splendid panoramas, can be done in late May and early June, when the trip is really the most pleasant, especially since rhododendrons are then in bloom along the lower trail.

However, the way goes on for those willing, following the ridge crest up

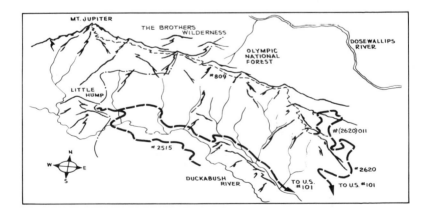

The Brothers from Mount Jupiter trail

and down, up and down, with more views, at 5 miles enters The Brothers Wilderness and finally climbs a very steep final mile to the summit, 7 miles, 5701 feet.

From the summit, or from the trail, the views are glorious. North beyond the Dosewallips is Mt. Constance, and south beyond the Duckabush are The Brothers. Westward is the grandeur of Olympic National Park. Eastward across Hood Canal and the Kitsap Peninsula are Seattle, the Space Needle, suburbia, smog, civilization.

Old road: 262
New road: (2620)011

79   LAKE CONSTANCE

Round trip to the lake 4 miles
Hiking time 7 hours
High point 4750 feet
Elevation gain 3300 feet
Hikable August through October
One day or backpack

USGS The Brothers and Tyler
  Peak
Park Service backcountry use
  permit required (from
  Hoodsport Ranger Station)

A classic tarn, the deep blue waters ringed by alpine trees and heather gardens and sheer cliffs of Mt. Constance. Mountain goats (an introduced and exotic species here—they don't really "belong") wander the precipices by day—and at night visit camps to scavenge goodies. But hikers must earn their passage to the secluded cirque the hard way, climbing 3300 feet in only 2 miles. The way trail is super-steep, dangerous in spots, and is not recommended for beginners or small children or the faint-hearted.

Drive US 101 along Hood Canal to the Dosewallips River road just north of Brinnon. Turn west 14 miles to .5 mile inside the park boundary and several wide spots that serve for the trailhead parking area at Constance Creek, elevation 1450 feet.

The first mile is brutal, virtually without switchbacks, gaining some 2000 feet to a short level stretch, and good forest camp, at the 1-mile marker. The second mile seems even steeper, though this is purely an optical illusion caused by the ladderways of tree roots and the short rock cliffs. Feet must be placed with care and hands used for balance. Caution is especially essential on the descent. At 2 miles, 4750 feet, the trail flattens into the cirque. Camping restrictions forced by popularity include a nightly limit of 20 campers (make reservations by calling or visiting the Park Service–Forest Service joint visitors' center at Hoodsport) and a ban on wood fires. Also, *use the privies.*

Impressive as is the lake, the truly awesome scenery lies higher, beyond the portals of what old-time Boy Scouts, feeling spooky, used to

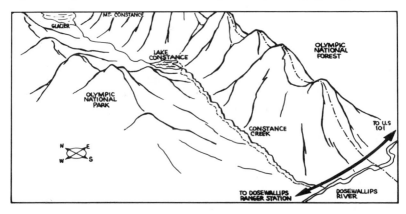

Lake Constance

call "Dead Man's Gap." Follow a boot-beaten climbers' track above the lake, up talus, through the gap into Avalanche Canyon, a mile-long glacier trough between the east and west peaks of Constance. Solemn and spectacular it is, a place of crags, cliffs, and screes, snowfields and moraines. Hikers can walk safely to the canyon head at about 6000 feet. Those with ice axes and experience in snow travel can climb easily to Crystal Pass and views down the glacier in Tunnel Creek.

The geology adds fascination. The weird, bumpy-looking walls of the canyon consist of "pillow lava" formed by molten rock erupting under the sea and cooling into these odd, rounded shapes. Heat and pressure metamorphosed limestone into pastel-colored rocks, often in variegated fault breccias of striking beauty. Hot mineralized solutions deposited green crystals of epidote intermixed with quartz and calcite.

ANDERSON GLACIER

Round trip to Anderson Glacier
  22½ miles
Allow 3 days
High point 5200 feet
Elevation gain 4000 feet

Hikable mid-July through
  October
USGS The Brothers and Mt. Steel
Park Service backcountry use
  permit required

Follow a long trail to the edge of one of the largest glaciers in the eastern Olympics. Enjoy glorious views down the Dosewallips River to Mt. Constance, over Anderson Pass to Mt. LaCrosse and White Mountain, down into the Enchanted Valley at the head of the Quinault River, and of course, across the Anderson Glacier to the summits of Mt. Anderson. In early August a wild array of flowers blooms, including small fields of lupine and paintbrush that stand out dramatically against the rugged background.

Drive US 101 along Hood Canal to just north of Brinnon and turn west on the Dosewallips River road, coming to the end of pavement in 4.7 miles, Elkhorn Campground junction at 10.7 miles, Constance Creek at 13.5 miles, and at 15 miles the road-end and trailhead, elevation 1540 feet.

The trail starts in deep forest with a showing of rhododendrons in late June, and after going up and down a bit reaches a junction at 1½ miles. Turn left to Dose Forks Camp and cross the river. At about 2½ miles the way again crosses the river, now the West Fork Dosewallips, this time on a bridge perched spectacularly some 100 feet above the water. The trail climbs steeply to dry forests high above the stream, which flows in so deep a gorge that often it cannot be heard.

The trail descends a bit to a welcome drink of water and campsites at 5 miles, then climbs again and with minor ups and downs reaches the

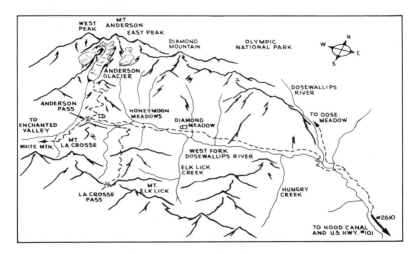

Mount Anderson from Anderson Pass

small opening of Diamond Meadow at 6¾ miles, 2692 feet. Pleasant campsites by the stream. At 7¼ miles the trail once more crosses the river and begins a steady ascent, at about 8 miles climbing steeply beside the raging torrent as it tumbles through a narrow gorge. At 8¾ miles, 3627 feet, the valley opens into the broad, flat expanse and good camps of Honeymoon Meadows, named years ago by a Seattle couple who long since have celebrated their golden wedding annniversary. (Here and above, stove-only camping. And the valley is infested with bears, so watch your groceries.) One final time the trail crosses the river, here a jump wide (a big jump), and ascends a rough path to Camp Siberia at 10 miles and Anderson Pass at 10½ miles, 4464 feet.

The Anderson Glacier Overlook way trail climbs steeply from the north side of the wooded pass, emerging from trees and in ¾ mile ending at a small tarn amid boulders and meadows. A few feet farther lead to the 5200-foot edge of an old moraine and the views.

The West Fork Dosewallips trail to Anderson Pass often is included in longer trips; a 27-mile one-way hike down Enchanted Valley (Hike 95); a 49-mile one-way hike to O'Neil Pass and out the Duckabush River (Hike 96); a 36½-mile one-way hike out the North Fork Skokomish River; and a 41-mile loop trip via O'Neil Pass and the upper Duckabush, returning to the Dosewallips with a grueling 3000-foot climb to LaCrosse Pass.

191

Avalanche lilies on Hayden Pass (John Spring photo)

HOOD CANAL
Olympic National Park

HAYDEN PASS

**Round trip to Hayden Pass 31
  miles**
Allow 3–4 days
High point 5847 feet
Elevation gain 4250 feet
Hikable July through October

**USGS Tyler Peak, The Brothers,
  Mt. Angeles**
**Park Service backcountry use
  permit required**

Miles of marvelous forest, then alpine meadows waist-deep in flowers, where fragrance makes the head swim on warm days, where a quiet hiker may see deer, elk, marmots, bear, and perhaps a goat on a high ridge. All this and impressive views too, plus numerous fine campsites at short intervals along the trail. The pass makes a superb round-trip destination or can be included in an across-the-Olympics journey to the Elwha River, or in a 10-day giant loop over Low Divide returning via Anderson Pass.

Drive US 101 along Hood Canal to the Dosewallips River road just north of Brinnon. Turn west 15.5 miles (the final 2 miles in the national park are steep and rough) to the road-end campground and trailhead, elevation 1540 feet.

A gentle 1½ miles through open forest with a dense ground cover of salal and rhododendron (the latter blooms in early July) lead to Dose Forks. A bit beyond is a junction with the trail to Anderson Pass (Hike 80); take the right fork and start climbing. At 2 miles note animal prints at a soda spring. Cross many little streams, nice spots for resting. At 2½ miles a sidetrail heads up to supremely scenic but far-above Constance Pass.

As the path ascends, Diamond Mountain appears across the river; from a well-marked point, see Hatana Falls. At about 8 miles the valley widens and the trail crosses a series of meadows. At 9 miles pass the Greywolf sidetrail and continue in steadily more open terrain, with wider views, to Dose Meadow at 13 miles, 4450 feet; no sign announces where you are, but a sidetrail here ascends rightward to Lost Pass.

Beyond the meadows is a small canyon which used to be crossed on a bridge; the creek-size river has a lion-size roar but makes no major difficulties. At 13½ miles, 4600 feet, the way enters the vast garden basin of the headwaters, surrounded by high peaks. The trail crosses the river one last time and switchbacks to Hayden Pass, 15½ miles, 5847 feet. In early summer a large, steep snowbank blocks the tread; be cautious.

Hayden Pass is the low point on the narrow ridge connecting Mt. Fromme and Sentinel Peak. North is Mt. Claywood, east are Wellesley Peak and the Dosewallips valley, south is glacier-covered Mt. Anderson, and west are the Bailey Range and distant Mt. Olympus.

Down from the pass 1 mile on the Elwha River side, just before the trail enters forest, find a delightful campsite by a bubbling creek.

For the across-the-Olympics hike, continue 9 miles and 4200 feet down from the pass to the Elwha River trail and then 17 miles more to the Whiskey Bend road-end (Hike 88).

No wood fires are permitted above 4000 feet; carry a stove or a lot of baloney sandwiches.

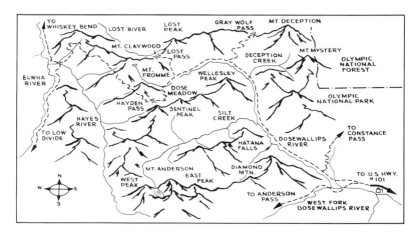

82   MARMOT PASS

Round trip to Marmot Pass 10½ miles
Hiking time 9 hours
High point 6000 feet
Elevation gain 3400 feet

Hikable July through mid-November
One day or backpack
USGS Tyler Peak

Before World War II, in an era when Boy Scouts were perhaps the principal wanderers of the Olympic wilderness, the "Three Rivers Hike" was among the most popular trips from old Camp Parsons. Thousands of Scouts now getting quite long in the tooth vividly recall their introduction to highlands on the grueling "Poop Out Drag," climbing steeply and endlessly upward along a sunbaked south slope, arriving in late afternoon at Camp Mystery, then taking an after-dinner walk through flower gardens and broad meadows to Marmot Pass and thrilling evening views down to shadowed forests of the Dungeness River, 3000 feet below, and beyond to Mt. Mystery, Mt. Deception, second highest in the Olympics, and the jagged line of The Needles, all etched in a sunset-colored sky.

Drive US 101 along Hood Canal to 9 miles south of the Quilcene Ranger Station and turn west on Penny Creek road. At 1.4 miles go left on a road signed "Quilcene Trail"; at 3.3 miles, right on road No. 2812; at 4.5 miles, right on No. 2812; at 10.5 miles, left on No. 2720, signed "Big Quilcene Trail 5"; and at 15.1 miles, just before crossing the river to a dead-end, find the start of Big Quilcene trail No. 833, elevation 2500 feet.

The trail follows the river through intensely green forest, all moss and ferns and lichen, crossing numerous step-across creeks, passing many close-up looks at the lovely river. At 2½ miles is Shelter Rock Camp, 3600 feet, and the last water for 2 miles.

Now the way turns steeply upward from big trees to little, the hot, dry scree alternating with flowers, of the famous (or infamous) Poop Out

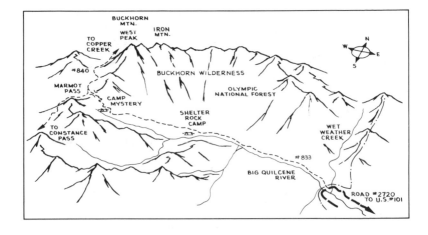

Warrior Peak and Mount Constance from Marmot Pass

Drag. At 4½ miles the suffering ends as the trail abruptly flattens out at Camp Mystery, 5400 feet, with two delightul springs and campsites in alpine trees. Except for snowmelt there is no water above, so this is the spot to camp.

The trail continues upward, passing under a cliff and opening into a wide, flat meadow, marmots whistling up a storm. At 5¼ miles, 6000 feet, the way attains Marmot Pass and panoramas westward—as well as back down east to Hood Canal.

The legendary Three Rivers Hike descended the trail 1½ miles to Boulder Shelter, followed Dungeness trail No. 833 to Home Lake and Constance Pass in Olympic National Park, climbed Del Monte Ridge, and plunged down the interminable short switchbacks of the Sunnybrook trail to the Dosewallips River trail and thence to the road. Using a two-car shuttle, the trip is still extremely popular.

Fine as the views are from Marmot Pass, nearby are even better ones. For a quick sample, scramble up the 6300-foot knoll directly south of the pass. For the full display, turn north of the pass on trail No. 840, leading to Copper Creek, follow it 1½ miles to just short of Buckhorn Pass, and find a path climbing to the 6950-foot west summit of Buckhorn Mountain. Especially striking are the dramatic crags of 7300-foot Warrior Peak and 7743-foot Mt. Constance, and the views north to the Strait of Juan de Fuca and Vancouver Island.

| Old road: | 2812 | 272 |
| New road: | 2812 | 2720 |

83 MOUNT TOWNSEND

Round trip 11 miles
Hiking time 6 hours
High point 6280 feet
Elevation gain 3500 feet

Hikable June through November
One day or backpack
USGS Tyler Peak

Climb to a northern outpost of the highlands. Look down to the Strait of Juan de Fuca, Puget Sound, Hood Canal, and across the water to Mt. Baker, Glacier Peak, and faraway Mt. Rainier. In the other direction, of course, see the Olympic Mountains. The steep southeast slopes of the trail route melt free of snow in early June, and usually only a few easy patches are encountered then. Mid-June is best, though, when the entire forest road is lined with rhododendron blossoms, spring flowers are blooming in the lowlands, and summer flowers on the south-facing rock gardens higher up.

Two popular trails lead to the summit of Mt. Townsend. The one from Townsend Creek, ascending the southeast side, is described here. The other, the Little Quilcene trail from Last Water Camp, is perhaps cooler walking in mid-summer but is not in as good shape.

Drive US 101 south from the Quilcene Ranger Station .9 mile. Turn west on a paved, unsigned road that eventually is revealed as road No. 2812. At all junctions stay with that number. At 13.6 miles turn left on road No. 2751. In .5 cliff-hanging mile is the road-end and trailhead, elevation about 2800 feet.

For the Last Water trail drive road No. 2812 another 5 miles and turn left on road No. 2909 for 2 miles, then left on road No. 2892 for 3 miles to the Little Quilcene River trailhead, elevation 4000 feet.

The Townsend Creek trail ascends steadily in timber 1½ miles, then opens out and steepens somewhat to Windy Camp, 2½ miles, about 5000 feet. Pleasant camping around little Windy Lake.

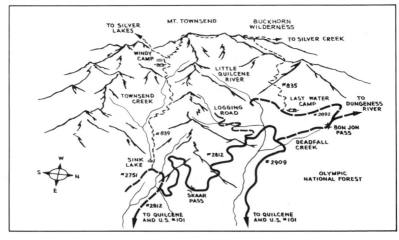

Headwaters of Silver Creek from Mount Townsend

The way continues upward in parkland with a scattering of small flower gardens. At just under 3 miles is a junction. The left fork climbs over a saddle, drops into Silver Creek, and climbs again to campsites at Silver Lakes, a sidetrip of 2½ miles each way; one small lake is on the trail and the other is hidden. The right fork heads up the mountain, topping the ridge at 4 miles, 6000 feet, then following the crest, passing 100 feet below the first summit at 4½ miles, and running to the most northerly part of the ridge and the second summit, connecting there with the Little Quilcene trail and a trail down to Silver Creek.

Which summit is the higher? They are so evenly matched—the north 6212 feet, the south 6280 but seeming lower—you must try both. Soak up the view over the waters to the Cascades and over the rolling meadow ridges of the Olympics. The rugged peaks to the south are Mt. Constance and its neighbors, and farther away, The Brothers.

Old road:	2812	2764	2909	2892
New road:	2812	2764	2909	2892

84   TUBAL CAIN MINE

**Round trip to Buckhorn Lake 12
   miles**
Hiking time 7 hours
High point 5300 feet
Elevation gain 2000 feet

Hikable July through October
One day or backpack
USGS Tyler Peak

In the 1890s the Tubal Cain Mine promoters began selling stock like crazy and hiring mules to haul tons of machinery, steel pipe, 10-inch wooden pipe, and such truck as elaborate bedsteads to the prospecting operation, hauling out just enough high-grade ore samples to keep the stock sales going. Originally supplies were brought in over Marmot Pass, but in the 1920s the route shifted to the Dungeness River, on a 14-mile trail starting at packer Charley Fritz's farm. The digging (first claimed to be for copper, later for manganese) pooped along by fits and starts until the 1950s and likely isn't ended yet; old mines never die, they just are

Tubal Cain Mine trail near Copper City

acquired by new stock salesmen. The frantically paced logging of recent decades has shortened the trail to a mere 3 miles, which ironically were rebuilt as a motorcycle expressway in time to be closed to mechanized vehicles by the 1984 Buckhorn Wilderness. Hike the trail in early July when rhododendrons are blooming the first 2 miles and the alpine meadows are flowered red, white, blue, and yellow.

Drive US 101 to .2 mile south of the entrance to Sequim Bay State Park, turn uphill on Louella Road .8 mile, and turn left on the Palo Alto road (which passes Charley Fritz's old farm). Paved road gives way to dirt and becomes road No. 2909. At 7.2 miles from the highway turn onto road No. 2950, cross the Dungeness River, and climb. At 12 miles go left, continuing on No. 2950. At 16.8 miles go left on road No. 2825, descending, and at 18.4 miles recross the Dungeness. At 22 miles reach the Tubal Cain trail parking lot, elevation 3300 feet.

In ¼ mile cross Silver Creek on a bridge built for wheels, enter Buckhorn Wilderness. Enjoy the lack of their racket as you pass through 10-foot rhododendrons, almost as high as the little firs. At 3 miles is the site of the Tubal Cain Mine. A shaft is located 50 feet above the trail; a bit farther on are pipes and rusted junk machinery. The buildings collectively known as Copper City have rotted into the soil or been burned up in campfires (or some of them, on a memorable Fourth of July in the 1930s, blown sky-high by larking youngsters who found the absent miners' cache of dynamite). At 3½ miles reach Copper Creek, 4300 feet, and camps.

Boulder-hop the creek to lush herbaceous meadows, the bright green gaudy-spotted with blossoms, and switchback a mile up steep slopes to about 5½ miles and an unmarked junction in a grove of trees.

The left fork goes in ½ mile of ups and downs to forest-ringed Buckhorn Lake, 5300 feet, 6 miles. Excellent camps near a stream a hundred feet above the lake.

The right fork is the entry to the sky, climbing meadows to the long, broad tundra ridge of Buckhorn Pass and its views of valleys and mountains and salt water, contouring rock gardens to Marmot Pass (Hike 82), and ascending Buckhorn Mountain.

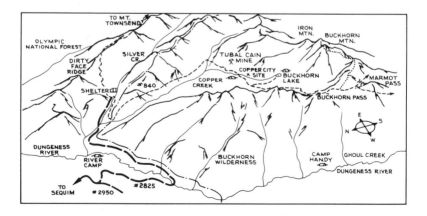

85   ROYAL BASIN

Round trip to Royal Lake 14 miles
Allow 2 days minimum
High point 5100 feet
Elevation gain 2600 feet

Hikable mid-July through
October
USGS Tyler Peak
Park Service backcountry use
permit required

Splendid forests and streams, an alpine lake and fields of flowers, surrounded by some of the highest and craggiest peaks in the Olympics. Allow plenty of time for the entry hike because the last several miles are rough and in places quite steep. Plan at least an extra day for roaming.

Drive US 101 westward toward Sequim. A few hundred feet before Sequim Bay State Park turn left on a gravel road .8 mile to the paved Palo Alto county road. (Alternatively, continue 1.5 miles on the highway and turn left on Palo Alto road; the gravel shortcut saves about 2 miles.) Turn left on the paved road, at 4 miles from the highway reaching the end of pavement and at 6.5 miles the end of the county road at a Forest Service junction. Turn left on road No. 2909, at 7.2 miles turn right on road No. 2950, and at 16.8 miles go left on road No. 2825. At 18.5 miles, beside the bridge over the river, find Dungeness River trail No. 833, elevation 2500 feet.

The trail follows the water—always within sound and often in sight. At 1 mile, 2700 feet, is a junction of streams and trails; take the right fork, Royal (originally Roy) Creek trail No. 832. In 2 miles enter a corner of Olympic National Park and at 3 miles reenter Buckhorn Wilderness. This far the way is entirely through forest, including beautiful specimens of fir, with a floor sometimes a soft mattress of moss and other times a broad green carpet of vanilla leaf. At around 4 miles the trail begins traversing small flower meadows, each larger than the last. The path also steepens and becomes rougher and at 4½ miles leaves wilderness to

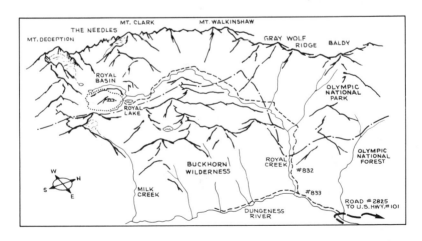

Peaks overlooking Royal Basin

reenter park. Ahead are glimpses of Greywolf Ridge and crags of The Needles.

The valley bends sharply southward and narrows and at about 6 miles, 4700 feet, the trail climbs a little cliff and enters the lower part of Royal Basin, covered with alpine trees and small meadows thick with scrub willow. The trail crosses Royal Creek and several tributaries on flimsy poles; note the milkiness of the main creek, which carries glacier-milled rock-flour. A final steep climb leads to Royal Lake, 7 miles, 5100 feet. On the far shores are numerous campsites in the woods. Near the sound of a waterfall directly west is a large camp under the huge overhang of Shelter Rock; to find it, follow a path around the upper end of the lake, then over a small knoll.

Several boot-beaten tracks lead to upper Royal Basin's high gardens. Any will do, but take care to skirt certain green, flat meadows which in fact are marshes. Make a grand tour to the very top of the basin. Below huge piles of moraine, find a tiny milk-blue lake fed by the small glacier on the side of 7788-foot Mt. Deception. Continue to the ridge crest and look down to the fairyland of Deception Basin.

86 MOUNT ANGELES— KLAHHANE RIDGE

Round trip 7 miles
Hiking time 4 hours
High point 5900 feet
Elevation gain 1200 feet

Hikable mid-July through
   October
One day
USGS Mt. Angeles and Port
   Angeles

The simultaneous views of glacier ice and salt waterways, the unusual geology underfoot (sedimentary strata tilted to the vertical), and the exuberance of flowers—these are reasons enough for Klahhane Ridge to be the most popular alpine hike in the Olympics. But the scene also has become famous (?) for mountain goats.

Drive south from Port Angeles 18 miles on the Olympic National Park highway to Hurricane Ridge Visitor Center and find the Lake Angeles–Klahhane Ridge trail at the east end of Big Meadow parking lot, elevation 5225 feet.

Paved path leads east around a green hill to gravel path, which in ½ mile yields to ordinary mountain trail winding 2 miles along Sunrise Ridge, on the crest and around knolls. Just before starting across the south side of Mt. Angeles, pass a boot-beaten path leading toward the summit, the climbers' route. At 2½ miles sniff contemptuously as you pass Switchback Trail. (This shortcut climbs a steep ½ mile from the highway, saving the "bother" of hiking 2 of the best alpine miles of the trip. Aren't you proud you didn't cheat?) Continue on, zigzagging 900 feet up to Klahhane Ridge, 5900 feet, 3½ miles, and a junction with the Lake Angeles trail. (By arranging transportation, you can descend this trail 1½ miles to Lake Angeles, 4196 feet, and proceed to the trailhead near Heart of the Hills Campground, 10 miles from Hurricane Ridge Lodge—a

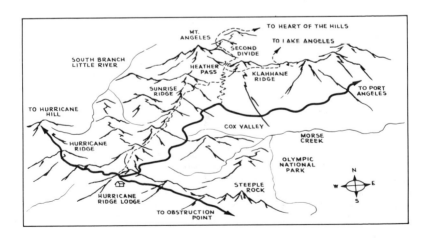

Klahhane Ridge

superb one-way, downhill, meadow-to-forest walk.)

The views from Klahhane are as good as views get: the ice of Mt. Olympus in one direction, in the other the Strait of Juan de Fuca, San Juan Islands, Vancouver Island, and the ice of Mt. Baker.

Now, about those goats. They are less native to the Olympics than bird-eating cats and rabbit-chasing dogs are to your house, for glaciological reasons never having made their way across the Puget Trough from the Cascades. In 1925 the state Department of Game, to repair nature's error, introduced a dozen mountain goats to the northern portion of what in the the next decade became a national park, no guns allowed. The bands grew slowly, and for years encounters were rare and exciting treats. Then, lacking predators, their populations exploded throughout the Olympics, they became camp pests, dangerous to hikers (when you meet one, keep well away, and get your close-up photos via telephoto; they are wild animals with sharp and harmful horns), and worse than that, a threat to endangered species of endemic plants that live no other place in the world, nor ever will if hooved to death here.

The Park Service has been compelled to take action. There is no intent (nor would it be practically possible) to eradicate goats from the park. The cheapest and most humane remedy would be to hire professional marksmen to thin out the bands. This having been vigorously protested, the Park Service is helicoptering animals off the ridge (where the goat census peaked at 250!) and trucking them to the Cascades; with no fear of humans, they are sitting ducks for the first guns they meet. The park bands reduced, much of the plant life will be restored, though years must pass before erosion scars are healed.

So much for blithely tampering with nature.

87 GRAND VALLEY

Round trip to Moose Lake 9 miles
Hiking time 6 hours
High point 6450 feet
Elevation gain 300 feet in, 1800
**   feet out**
Hikable July through October

One day or backpack
USGS Mt. Angeles
Park Service backcountry use
**   permit required**

A Grand Valley it surely is, with three lakes and a half-dozen ponds in glacier-scooped bowls, but it would better be called "Kingdom of Marmots." There are meadows to roam and rushing streams and views to admire. However, the abundant wildlife is the outstanding feature: an occasional goat, numerous deer and grouse, and an unbelievable number of whistlers.

This is an upside-down trip—the trail starts high and descends to the valley; the hard hauling is on the return. Usually open in July, after a winter of heavy snow the road may not open until August; ask the rangers before setting out.

Drive US 101 to Port Angeles and turn south 17 miles on the Olympic National Park highway to Hurricane Ridge. Just before the lodge turn left on a narrow and scenic dirt road through parklands along the ridge crest. In 8.5 miles, on the side of Obstruction Peak, is the road-end, elevation 6200 feet.

The drive is beautiful and so is the trail south along the meadow crest

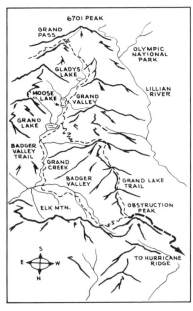

Olympic marmot

Camping in Grand Valley

of Lillian Ridge a mile, with views over Elwha River forests to Mt. Olympus, then swinging around rocky slopes of a small peak to a notch in the ridge, 6450 feet. Now the way drops steeply down slate screes and lush flowers to open forest on the floor of Grand Valley, and a junction at 3½ miles, 5000 feet.

The left fork leads in ¼ mile to Grand Lake, 4750 feet, then descends Grand Creek to 4000 feet and climbs through Badger Valley to Obstruction Peak, reached in 5 miles from the junction. (The "badgers" actually are marmots; listen for their whistles.) This route makes an excellent loop-trip return to the road.

The right fork ascends ½ mile to Moose Lake, 5100 feet, and another ½ mile to little Gladys Lake. There are nice camps near Moose and Grand Lakes (remember the minimum camping distance from lakes or streams is 100 feet) but for privacy scout around secret nooks in the vicinity of Gladys.

For more alpine wanderings, continue on the trail to 6300-foot Grand Pass, 6½ miles from Obstruction Point, then scramble up Peak 6701 to the west, with views to the Bailey Range and Mt. Olympus and Mt. Anderson and more.

If the weather turns bad when it's time to go home, keep in mind that the last mile along Lillian Ridge can be a battle for survival, even in July and August. In such case it is wise to return via Badger Valley, several miles longer but mostly protected from the killing winds. Moreover, a wood fire is permitted at one site in Badger Valley.

WHISKEY BEND TO
LOW DIVIDE

Round trip to Low Divide 57½
  miles
Allow a week or more
High point 3602 feet
Elevation gain about 2500 feet,
  plus many ups and downs
Hikable June through October

USGS Mt. Angeles; Mt. Steel and
  Mt. Christie
Park Service backcountry use
  permit required

No whiskey, but a lot of waterfalls and forest scenery, can be found on
the 28-mile Elwha River trail from Whiskey Bend to Low Divide. The
valley is very heavily traveled in summer, especially below Elkhorn, but
the natural beauty and historical interest more than compensate for
crowds. Spend a day or weekend on the lower trail—or spend a week hiking the complete trail, loitering at lovely spots, taking sidetrips. Before
setting out be sure to read Bob Wood's delightful book, *Across the Olympic Mountains: the Press Expedition, 1889–90.*

Drive US 101 west from Port Angeles 8 miles and turn left on the
paved Elwha River road 2 miles to the national park boundary. At 2.1
miles from the boundary, just past the Elwha Ranger Station, turn left
on the Whiskey Bend road and drive 5 miles (sometimes rough and steep)
to the road-end parking area, elevation 1100 feet.

The trail is wide and relatively level, with occasional glimpses of the
river far below, to Michael's (Cougar Mike's) Cabin at 1½ miles. Here a
⅓-mile sidetrail descends to the old homestead of Humes Ranch, where
elk may sometimes be seen, mainly from late fall to spring.

At 4½ miles, 1273 feet, is Lillian Camp beside the Lillian River. Pause
for refreshment because the next stretch is the toughest of the trip,
climbing 700 feet from the hot, dry Lillian Grade through an old burn,
then dropping for the first time to the Elwha River at about 8 miles, 1242
feet. The trail goes up and down, never near the river very long, to

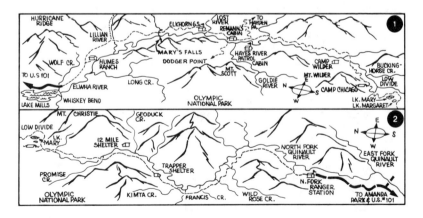

Quinault rain forest

Mary's Falls, 8¾ miles, and a nice view of the falls. Now the way climbs again, passing a ¼-mile sidetrip to secluded Canyon Camp, and at 11½ miles, 1400 feet, reaches Elkhorn Guard Station.

The trail crosses an alder bottom where elk or deer may be seen and passes an old summer-home cabin of prepark days—Remanns' Cabin (13 miles, 1450 feet)—and climbs again and drops again into Press Valley. At the upper end of the valley, 16¾ miles, 1685 feet, are Hayes River Camp and Hayes River Patrol Cabin, built in 1969 by 40 volunteer boys enrolled in the Student Conservation Program. Here is a junction with the Hayden Pass trail (Hike 81).

At 21 miles, 1900 feet, is Camp Wilder. Easily cross a footlog over Buckinghorse Creek and at 26 miles reach Chicago Camp, 2099 feet, a jumping-off point for Mt. Olympus climbers. The trail now leaves the valley bottom and switchbacks in forest to the meadows of Low Divide, 28¾ miles, 3602 feet, and there meets the North Fork Quinault River trail.

To complete the classic Press Expedition cross-Olympics journey, continue from the pass 18 miles down the valley to the North Fork Quinault River road-end, for a total of 45 miles.

89 APPLETON PASS

Round trip to pass 14½ miles
Hiking time 9 hours
High point 5000 feet
Elevation gain 3300 feet
Hikable mid-July through
**   October (or until road is closed)**

One day or backpack
USGS Mt. Carrie
Park Service backcountry use
**   permit required**

One of the most popular trails in Olympic National Park climbs to green meadows sprinkled with flowers, to views of High Divide and Mt. Carrie, and to possible extensions of the route to near and far places.

Drive US 101 west from Port Angeles about 9 miles and turn left on Upper Elwha River road, paved all the way, 10.5 miles to the road-end, elevation 1840 feet. Walk the abandoned road 2 miles to Boulder Creek Campground (site of Olympic Hot Springs), elevation 2000 feet.

From the upper end of the campground the trail sets out in nice big trees growing from a ground cover of moss. The calypso orchids stage an annual riot hereabouts, usually in early June or so. At a junction in ½ mile, keep straight. The first mile is a breeze with only minor ups and downs. Then the trail crosses West Fork Boulder Creek and the work begins, the way climbing past two waterfalls to South Fork Boulder Creek. An unusual feature of the trail is the superb quality of the bridges and puncheon, which were built by meticulous craftspeople, including close relatives and friends of one of the co-authors. The path presents no problems but steepness until about 4000 feet, where mud grows deep and lush vegetation crowds in. At 5 miles are snow patches that may last all summer (ice axes advised for early-summer hikers). At 6 miles the trail tops 5000-foot Appleton Pass.

Views from here being limited, take an unsigned way trail on the east side of the pass and follow the ridge crest upward, through alpine forest

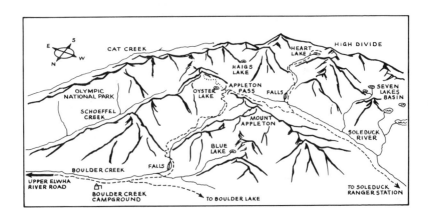

Mount Olympus from near Oyster Lake

past tiny Oyster Lake, into green meadows, and in 1½ miles to a 5500-foot viewpoint overlooking Cat Creek to glacier-draped Mt. Carrie.

The first 3 miles of the trail have several small camps. Camping is superb along the ridge, though there is only snow for water and stoves should be used.

From Appleton Pass the trail descends in 2¼ miles to the Soleduck River trail, reached at 6½ miles from Sol Duc Hot Springs.

90 PYRAMID MOUNTAIN

Round trip 7 miles
Hiking time 4 hours
High point 3100 feet
Elevation gain 2400 feet

Hikable late May through October
One day
USGS Lake Crescent

From Lake Crescent a delightful trail ascends magnificent forest to the 3100-foot site of a World War II airplane spotter's post. No enemy aircraft to watch for now except our own military jets, screaming over the ridges and scaring the breakfasts out of hikers, but there are views of lake and mountains. A delightful trip, yes, but marred by a logging road to the very boundary of Olympic National Park. Ignore it, if you can.

Drive US 101 west from Port Angeles to the west end of Lake Crescent and turn right on the road signed "Fairholm Campground." Drive 3.2 miles to a spacious parking lot, elevation 700 feet. Walk the road back a couple of hundred yards to find the trail on the uphill side.

After a moderate start, gaining only 400 feet in the first mile, at 1½ miles the way steepens, crosses several small streams (perhaps dry by late summer), and goes through beautiful fir trees. The tread is mostly well-graded and wide but on crossings of steep shale narrows to meager inches.

At 2½ miles the trail switchbacks to a saddle in the ridge marking the boundary between Olympic National Park and Olympic National Forest. A logging road here is a jolting reminder of the different objectives of park and forest. It also is shocking evidence of a contempt for wilderness—the road could just as well have been built farther below the ridge crest, out of sight, not disturbing the mood. Even though the forest probably will be clearcut to the park boundary, there was no need to put a permanent road that close—the logging could be done from temporary roads that afterward are put to bed. As it is, some hikers surely are going to feel so disheartened they'll drive the road and throw away the best part of the trip, making it a mere stroll.

From the saddle the trail stays on the national forest side of the ridge, generally a few feet from the crest. At 3½ miles, 3100 feet, it ends at an abandoned cabin perched atop a cliff dropping off on three sides. Here

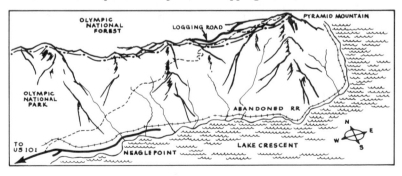

Lake Crescent and Storm King Mountain from Pyramid Mountain

and in many other places in the Olympics, during World War II, spotters lived the year around, watching for Japanese aircraft coming to attack Seattle and Bremerton. The view must have been better then; now greenery has encroached and one must peek around trees and shrubs to look down on the lake. On a sunny day the waters are dotted with boats. Directly across the valley is Storm King Mountain, but trees make it hard to see.

Mount Olympus and avalanche lilies on High Divide

STRAIT OF JUAN DE FUCA
Olympic National Park

HIGH DIVIDE

Round trip 20 miles
Allow 3 days
High point 5474 feet
Elevation gain 4000 feet
Hikable August through October

USGS Bogachiel Peak and Mt.
Carrie
Park Service backcountry use
permit required

Soleduck forests, tarns and gardens of Seven Lakes Basin, meadows of the High Divide, and views across the green gulf of the Hoh River to glaciers of Mt. Olympus and far west to the Pacific Ocean. The trail is busy and the lakes crowded—sad to say, some are actually polluted—but the country is big and beautiful and offers a variety of wanderings short and long. By planning only to *look* at lakes and not camp by them— alternative sites are numerous—hikers can enjoy solitude even now, when the fame of the area draws thousands of visitors annually. A loop trip is recommended as a sampler of the riches. (Actually, the bio-welfare of Seven Lakes Basin and the High Divide demands that the amount of camping in the fragile terrain be reduced, with more emphasis on day visits from camps in valley forests.)

Drive US 101 west from Lake Crescent (Fairholm) 2 miles to the Soleduck River road. Turn left 14.2 miles to the road-end and trailhead, elevation 2000 feet.

The trail ascends gently in splendid old forest 1 mile to the misty and mossy gorge of Soleduck Falls. Close by is the junction, 1950 feet, with the Deer Lake trail—see the concluding segment of the clockwise loop described here.

The Soleduck trail continues up the valley of gorgeous trees, passes the Appleton Pass trail at 5 miles, 3000 feet, and soon thereafter crosses the river and climbs steeply to grasslands and silver forest of Soleduck Park and Heart Lake, 7 miles, 4800 feet.

Shortly above, at 8½ miles, the way attains the 5100-foot crest of the High Divide, and a junction. The left fork runs the ridge 3 miles to a dead end on the side of Cat Peak, offering close looks at the Bailey and Olympus Ranges.

Turn west on the right fork into a steady ridge-top succession of views far down to trees of the Hoh valley and across to ice of Mt. Olympus. At 10½ miles a sidetrail descends 1½ miles left to 4500-foot Hoh Lake, and from there to the Hoh River (Hike 93). Here, too, a path climbs a bit to the 5474-foot summit of Bogachiel Peak and the climax panoramas. Plan to spend a lot of time gazing the full round of the compass.

The route swings along the side of the peak, at 11½ miles passing the sidetrail to Seven Lakes Basin (often snowbound on the north side until mid-August), and traverses Bogachiel Ridge above the greenery (and often, a band of elk) in Bogachiel Basin. Snowfields linger late on this stretch and may be troublesome or dangerous for inexperienced hikers who try the trip too early in the summer.

The trail contours the ridge above the Bogachiel River almost 2 miles, then in subalpine trees drops to Deer Lake at 3500 feet and a junction with the Bogachiel River trail (Hike 92) at 15½ miles. Past the lake, the trail descends in lush forest to Soleduck Falls at 19 miles and in another mile to the road.

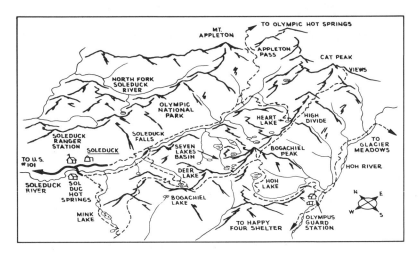

92 BOGACHIEL RIVER

**Round trip from park boundary
to Bogachiel Shelter 8 miles**
Hiking time 5 hours
High point 560 feet
Elevation gain 260 feet
Hikable March through
November
One day or backpack
USGS Olympic National Park or
Spruce Mountain

**One-way trip to Sol Duc Hot
Springs via Deer Lake 30½ miles**
Allow 2–3 days
High point 4304 feet
Elevation gain 4000 feet
Hikable July through October
Park Service backcountry use
permit required

A beautiful hike through large old trees, rain-forest foliage, and luxuriant mosses. In autumn, the vine maple, alder, and bigleaf maple stage a glorious color show. Elk, deer, cougar, bear, and other animals may be seen by quiet and lucky hikers. A late-fall or winter visitor usually has the forest all to himself, the only footprints on the trail those of elk. The valley offers a superb day trip for virtually any time of year, or a weekend for more extended enjoyment of wilderness greenery and streams, or a long, magnificent approach to alpine climaxes of the High Divide.

Drive US 101 to Bogachiel State Park. On the north side of the river go east on the Bogachiel River road, passing several sideroads to homesteads; keep left at each intersection. At 3.6 miles leave the main road and drive another mile to a gate and parking area, 4.6 miles from the highway, elevation 350 feet.

The trail descends ¼ mile, intersects and follows an old logging road 2½ miles to the park boundary and 1½ miles more in the park. Amid second-growth forest (logging done during World War II on the grounds of "national emergency") look for giant stumps with springboard holes in both sides. Then virgin forest begins.

Bogachiel Shelter (emergency use only) and the old guard station, rebuilt by the Student Conservation Program, are 4 miles from the park boundary and make a good lunch stop and turnaround point for day hikers.

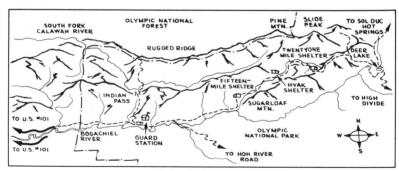

Bogachiel River (John Spring photo)

Near the shelter a branch trail climbs north over 1041-foot Indian Pass and drops to the Calawah River; at 6¼ miles another sidetrail fords the river and climbs over the ridge south to the Hoh River road.

The valley path continues gently in lovely forest, never far from the river and sometimes beside it, to Flapjack Camp at 8¼ miles. At about 12 miles the river forks. While the trail follows the North Fork, the narrow but pristine main river valley can be explored on a sidetrip for 6 miles if you don't mind wading creeks and scrambling over high banks and fallen trees.

At 14¾ miles are Fifteenmile Shelter and a bridge crossing the stream. At 15½ miles is Hyak Shelter, where the valley narrows to a slot, and at 18½ miles Twentyone Mile Shelter, 2214 feet. At around 21 miles the trail abandons gentility, steeply ascends a dry hillside above the North Fork headwaters to 4300-foot Little Divide, then drops to Deer Lake at 24 miles, and climbs in parklands to the meadow crest of the High Divide. For alternative exits to Sol Duc Hot Springs, see Hike 91.

215

93 HOH RIVER

Round trip to Happy Four Camp
  11½ miles
Hiking time 6 hours
High point 800 feet
Elevation gain 225 feet
Hikable March through
  November
One day or backpack
USGS Mt. Tom

Round trip to Glacier Meadows 37
  miles
Allow 3 days
High point 4200 feet
Elevation gain 3700 feet
Hikable mid-July through
  October
USGS Olympic National Park or
  Mt. Tom and Mt. Olympus
Park Service backcountry use
  permit required

From around the world travelers are drawn to the Hoh River by the fame of the Olympic rain forest. Most of the 100,000 annual visitors are richly satisfied by the self-guiding nature walks at the road-end, but

Hoh River rain forest

more ambitious hikers can continue for miles on the nearly flat trail through huge trees draped with moss and then climb to alpine meadows and the edge of the Blue Glacier.

Drive US 101 to the Hoh River road and turn east 19 miles to the Hoh Ranger Station and Campground, elevation 578 feet. The hike begins on the nature trail starting at the visitor center; before setting out, study the museum displays explaining the geology, climate, flora, and fauna.

The way lies amid superb, large specimens of Douglas fir, western hemlock, Sitka spruce, and western red cedar, groves of bigleaf maple swollen with moss, and shrubs and ferns. Gravel bars and cold rapids of the river are never far away, inviting sidetrips. Here and there are glimpses upward to snows of Mt. Tom and Mt. Carrie. In winter one may often see bands of Roosevelt elk; were it not for their constant grazing, the relatively open forest floor would be a dense jungle. Beside the Hoh River at 3¾ miles is the park's largest known Sitka spruce, 51½ feet in circumference; the winter of 1975 it toppled, but it's impressive even lying down.

Any distance can make a full day, what with long, lingering pauses. Happy Four Camp, at 5¾ miles, elevation 800 feet, is a logical turn-around for a day hike and also a good campsite for backpackers.

The trail remains level to the next camp at Olympus Guard Station, 9 miles, 948 feet. At 9¾ miles is a junction with the trail to High Divide (Hike 91). The valley trail then climbs a bit to the bridge over the spectacular canyon of the Hoh at 13¼ miles, 1400 feet, leaves the Hoh valley, and climbs more to forest-surrounded Elk Lake, 15 miles, 2500 feet. (Crowded camping, stove required.)

Now the grade becomes steep, ascending through steadily smaller trees, with views across Glacier Creek of snows and cliffs, to Glacier Meadows, 17¼ miles, 4200 feet. (Stove camping only.) Wander a short way in flowers and parkland to a viewpoint near the foot of the Blue Glacier, where torrents pour down ice-polished slabs to the forest below. Or follow the trail ½ mile to the end on the bouldery crest of a lateral moraine. Admire crevasses and icefalls of the glacier, and the summit tower of 7965-foot Mt. Olympus.

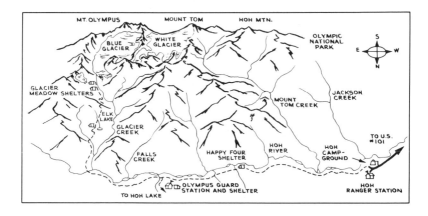

94 COLONEL BOB MOUNTAIN

Round trip, north side, 14½ miles
Allow 2 days
High point 4492 feet
Elevation gain 4220 feet
Hikable July through
mid-October
USGS Quinault Lake, Grisdale,
Mt. Christie

Round trip, south side, 8.4 miles
Hiking time 7 hours
Elevation gain 3500 feet
One day or backpack

Climb to a western outpost of the Olympic Mountains, a former lookout
site with views of Olympics nearby and, farther off, volcanoes of the
Cascades—St. Helens, Adams, and Rainier. There's water to see, too—
look down on sparkling Quinault Lake and out to the Pacific Ocean, particularly spectacular with the sun dunking into it of an evening.

There are two ways, both very steep, to Colonel Bob. The south approach gains 3500 feet; the north climbs 4220 feet and is 3 miles longer.

For the north side drive US 101 to near its crossing of the Quinault
River and turn east on the South Shore road. In 2.5 miles pass the
Quinault Ranger Station and at 6 miles spot a sign, "Colonel Bob Trail"
(No. 851). Turn in on a narrow road which promptly opens to a large
parking lot, elevation 270 feet.

The trail climbs through beautiful rain forest in long, sweeping
switchbacks, then sidehills, still going steadily up. At 3 miles is a crossing of Ewell's Creek and soon after are campsites of Mulkey Shelter,
2550 feet. Now the way switchbacks steeply to a 3250 foot pass and drops
a bit, at 5½ miles reaching a junction, 2900 feet, with the trail from the
south.

For the south-side approach to this junction, drive US 101 north 25½
miles from Hoquiam and turn east on road No. 22, signed "Donkey Creek
Road, Humptulips Guard Station." At 8.2 miles, where pavement ends,
turn left on road No. 2302, signed "Campbell Tree Grove Campground,"
and proceed 11 miles to a sign, "Petes Creek Trail" (No. 858), near the

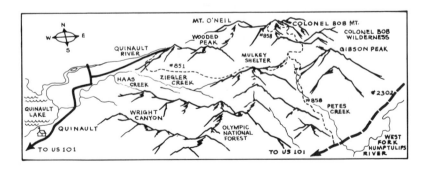

Near summit of Colonel Bob Mountain

crossing of Petes Creek, elevation 1000 feet.

The trail starts on the uphill side of the road and is steadily steep and in places rocky. At 1 mile is a crossing of Petes Creek, underground here most of the year. At 2 miles is a small camp, beyond which is Gibson Slide and then, at 2½ miles, the junction.

About 1 mile beyond, at 6½ miles from the north trailhead and 3⅓ from the south, is Moonshine Flats, with all-year water, the most popular camp on the route. At 1¾ miles from the junction, the way emerging from forest into flowers, is the summit, the last few feet to the top blasted from rock.

Few traces of the old lookout cabin remain on the 4492-foot summit. But the views are glorious as ever. For sunset watching, camps can be found ¼ mile back, 200 feet below the trail, on a wide, rocky bench covered with snow much of the summer. Bring a stove for cooking; melt snow for water.

Old road: 220 2302
New road: 22 2302

95 ENCHANTED VALLEY

Round trip 27 miles
Allow 2–3 days
High point 1957 feet
Elevation gain 1050 feet, plus ups
  and downs
Hikable March through
  December

USGS Olympic National Park or
  Mt. Christie and Mt. Steele
Park Service backcountry use
  permit required

Walk beside the river in open alder and maple forest, and miles through cathedrallike fir forest where future generations of loggers will come to see what their grandfathers meant when they boasted of big trees. The climax is Enchanted Valley, a large alpine cirque ringed by 3000-foot cliffs. The trail has many ups and downs and during rainy spells is a muddy mess, but in such country, who can complain?

Drive US 101 to the south-side Lake Quinault road. Turn easterly, skirting the lake and winding up the valley. Pavement ends at 12 miles. In 13 miles pass the North Fork bridge and at 18 miles Graves Creek Campground. Continue on the final narrow road to the trailhead 18.5 miles from US 101, elevation 907 feet. (*Note:* Fall storms often flood out the road past the bridge, and repairs sometimes cannot be completed until late spring or early summer. In such cases the round-trip distance is 14 miles longer.)

The trail crosses Pony Bridge over the Quinault River at 3 miles; the lovely canyon under the bridge is worth a trip in itself. In another ½ mile climb around the canyon and drop back to the river. For the next 10 miles the way alternates, up and down, between flat bottoms (alders and maples) and terraces several hundred feet above the river (groves of tall fir and cedar). With any luck a hiker should see elk. At 7 miles pass a junction to O'Neil Creek Camp, ¼ mile off the main track.

All along are tantalizing glimpses of peaks above, but at about 10½ miles the change from lowlands to alpine is dramatic. Suddenly one leaves deep forest and bursts into the mountain world of rock and ice. To

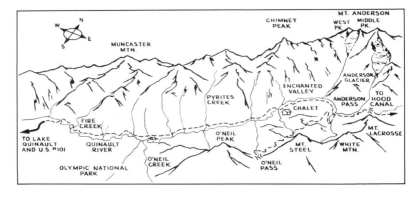

the left are cliffs of 6911-foot Chimney Peak. To the right is 6400-foot White Mountain. Both are dominated by the twin peaks of Mt. Anderson, divided by a small glacier: the sharp pyramid is 7366-foot West Peak, the highest point; the more massive peak in the middle is 7321 feet.

Coming down to earth, the valley has widened out. The lower part is floored with dense brush but farther up are flower fields. At 13½ miles cross the Quinault River, now a small creek. Walk a short bit through meadows to the three-story Enchanted Valley Chalet, built in 1930 as a commercial hotel and now maintained by the Park Service as a public shelter. The structure often is full (only part of the lower floor is open to camping) so be prepared to camp out. Be sure to carry a stove; cooking facilities are limited in the chalet and wood may be wet outside. Those unable to do the full 11 miles in a single day can stop overnight at any of a number of camps along the way.

Beyond the chalet the trail climbs 2500 feet in 5 miles to 4500-foot Anderson Pass, at 2 miles passing the largest known living western hemlock, 8 feet, 8 inches in diameter. It then descends the West Fork Dosewallips River 10 miles to the road (Hike 80). Another trail leads to O'Neil Pass and Hart, Marmot, and Lake LaCrosse (Hike 96).

What's the best season for the trip? Well, some winters there is little snow in the lower valley, which thus can be walked in December or March when hardly any other country is open. Early spring is wonderful, when birds are singing, and shrubs and maples are exploding with new leaves, and yellow violet and oxalis are blooming, and waterfalls and avalanches tumble and slide down cliffs. So is summer, when alders and maples canopy the valley bottoms in cool green. But fall is also glorious, with bigleaf maples yellowing and the trail lost in fallen leaves. Better try it in all seasons.

Oxalis

96 LAKE LACROSSE— O'NEIL PASS

One-way trip to Lake LaCrosse:
via Quinault River and O'Neil
Pass 26¾ miles
High point 4900 feet
Elevation gain 4000 feet
Allow 5 days minimum, by any
route

Hikable mid-July through
September
USGS Mt. Steel
Park Service backcountry use
permit required

In the heart of the Olympic wilderness, 16 miles from the nearest road, a group of beautiful alpine lakes sparkle amid a wonderland of heather and huckleberries. Quicker ways of reaching the lakes are mentioned in the last paragraph, but the one described here is the classic approach, via O'Neil Pass, on one of the most spectacular trails in the national park, traversing ridges high above the Enchanted Valley of the Quinault, with many and magnificent views and flower fields.

To reach the O'Neil Pass trail, hike 17 miles and gain 2400 feet up the Enchanted Valley (Hike 95) to the beginning at about 3400 feet (incorrectly shown as 3100 feet on the USGS map).

The O'Neil Pass trail starts from the Enchanted Valley trail beside a small torrent and heads westward and up, in a few yards going by a small camp. The way alternates between forest and wide-view meadows. At 1 mile are campsites and a crossing of White Creek; a hillside beyond gives the best look at Mt. Anderson.

At 1½ miles is a mountain hemlock with a sign saying it is 6 feet, 3 inches in diameter and 136 feet tall—a midget compared to the lowland species of hemlock but huge at this elevation. At 2 miles is an Alaska cedar identified as 7 feet, 6 inches in diameter and 114 feet tall.

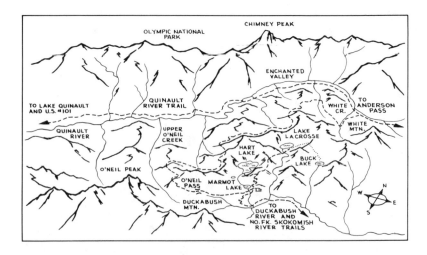

Lake LaCrosse

The trail climbs to 4500 feet and then contours for miles, mainly in grass and blossoms. Directly across the valley is Chimney Peak, an impressive 6911 feet high. Views are breathtaking down the Quinault River to Lake Quinault and, if lucky, the ocean. The trail drops a bit, rounds a shoulder of the ridge, and ascends to O'Neil Pass, 7½ miles (25 miles from the road), 4900 feet, and close-ups of Mt. Duckabush. Still in meadows, the way descends to Marmot Lake, 8½ miles, 4400 feet. The O'Neil Pass trail ends here in a junction with the Duckabush River trail (Hike 77).

Scattered through higher gardens are Hart Lake, Lake LaCrosse, and Buck Lake. To get there, find the trail behind Marmot Lake Shelter and switchback upward ¾ mile to a junction. The left fork contours ½ mile to Hart Lake, enclosed on three sides by vertical cliffs; good camps. The right fork continues ¾ mile uphill to Lake LaCrosse, 4800 feet, perhaps the most splendid alpine lake in the Olympics, with views across the water to massive 6233-foot Mt. Duckabush and more graceful 6300-foot Mt. Steel. Another mile farther is Buck Lake, too small for fish and thus more private; there is no trail, but an experienced hiker can find the way from Lake LaCrosse west over a 5500-foot saddle and down to the 5000-foot shores. Camping is great at all the lakes.

The camping is stove only, no wood fires, at Marmot, Hart, and LaCrosse lakes and O'Neil Pass. Marmot Lake is the most crowded.

The lakes can be approached in various other ways. For one, hike the Dosewallips trail (Hike 80) and drop over Anderson Pass 1½ miles, losing 1100 feet, to the start of the O'Neil Pass trail. Or, hike directly to the lakes by way of the Duckabush River trail 20 miles to Marmot Lake, gaining 4500 feet including some major ups and downs, and some difficult river crossings. For another, hike the North Fork Skokomish River trail (Hike 74) 19½ miles to Marmot Lake, gaining 5200 feet counting ups and downs. The lakes can also be included in imaginative one-way and loop trips.

97 POINT OF THE ARCHES

Round trip to Point of the Arches	**One day or backpack**
7 miles	**USGS Cape Flattery and Ozette**
Hiking time 4 hours	**Lake**
High point 150 feet	**Park Service backcountry use**
Hikable all year	**permit required**

Here, perhaps, is the most scenic single segment of the Washington ocean coast, with needlelike sea stacks, caves, and arches to explore, tidal pools, and miles of sand beaches. Once threatened with road building and subdivision, in 1976 Shi-Shi Beach and the Point were added to the wilderness-ocean section of Olympic National Park.

Drive from Port Angeles on narrow, tortuous Highway 112 to the Makah village of Neah Bay. At the west end of town turn left and follow signs to "Air Force Base and Ocean Beaches," crossing and recrossing a private logging road—stay on the public road. In 3 miles turn left over the Waatch River on a concrete bridge, again avoid the private road in favor of the public road, in about 6 miles cross the Sooes River, and pass a cluster of Makah homes on Mukkaw Bay at 6.5 miles. Beyond the settlement the road climbs into woods above the beach and in 1 mile deteriorates rapidly. Park either near the houses or where the road gets sloppy. Overnight hikers do best to ask at one of the houses for parking space for a fee; car looting is a problem here.

The parking area and road are on the Makah Indian Reservation. The ocean beach and all adjacent land belong to the Makahs so private property rules apply.

The undrivable road over Portage Head is pleasant walking under a canopy of trees. During wet weather be prepared for much mud. In about 1 mile push through the roadside brush for dramatic looks down to the surf. At 1½ miles, where the road comes to the edge of the bluff for the first unobstructed views of the ocean, are two "trails," side by side. The first drops like a shot to the north end of Shi-Shi Beach and is slippery and even scary. The other, several yards away, is steep enough but descends amid trees that provide handholds and a feeling of security. (If the tide is high, follow the "road," which dwindles to a track and in a mile nearly touches the beach.)

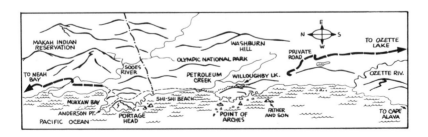

Point of Arches

A short sidetrip north from the foot of the trail is the south end of Portage Head, with spectacular sea stacks, tidal pools, and a shipwreck. For Point of the Arches, hike about 2 miles south on the beach, leaving the reservation, passing a number of good camps (the most reliable source of water in summer is Petroleum Creek). The long string of stacks and islands can be reached and explored at very low tide; the going is rough over sharp and slippery rocks and involves some wading.

It is possible to hike south toward Cape Alava, but some headlands must be rounded at low tide (in stormy weather the tide may never get low enough) and others must be climbed over on mean and nasty bushwhacking routes. About 6 miles from Point of the Arches is the Ozette River; a bit north of the river a road (closed to public vehicles) leads inland 4½ miles to Ozette Lake. In dry spells in calm weather at low tide the Ozette River may be only knee-deep, permitting sturdy hikers to wade and continue to Cape Alava (Hike 98).

98
CAPE ALAVA— SAND POINT LOOP

Loop trip 9½ miles
Hiking time 6 hours
High point 170 feet
Elevation gain about 500 feet,
  including ups and downs

Hikable all year
One day or backpack
USGS Ozette Lake

Two trails from Ozette Lake to the ocean, plus the connecting stretch of Olympic National Park wilderness beach, make a magnificent loop hike for one day or several, for winter as well as summer, passing a deserted homestead, the site of an Indian village, and miles of wild surf.

Drive from Port Angeles on Highway 112 past Sekiu and turn left on the Ozette Lake road to the road-end ranger station, campground, and parking lot where the Ozette River flows from the lake, elevation 36 feet. Both trails depart from the same point and the loop is equally good in either direction. Begin by crossing the bridge over the river; on the far side the trails diverge.

If the counterclockwise loop is chosen, take the Cape Alava trail, which goes a short bit on abandoned road and plunges into dense greenery of salal, hemlock, and other shrubs and trees. The path is sometimes flat, sometimes up and down a little, much of the way on planks—which may puzzle and irritate summertime hikers but not those who do the trip in

Common murre

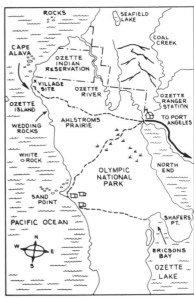

Pictographs near Cape Alava

fall or spring when all the bare ground is black muck, or in winter when every depression is feet deep in water. Walk with caution—the planks can be slippery and the memories of the average hiker include a pratfall or two. Lug soles are not recommended; ripple or smooth rubber soles give better traction.

At 2 miles the route opens out magically into a broad bog—Ahlstroms Prairie, partly a one-time lake filled in by natural processes, partly a pasture cleared early in the century by a homesteader, Lars Ahlstrom. At the far side of the bog are remnants of a cabin and outbuildings. There are ghosts here. Pause a while to meet them.

Again the trail enters greenery, and now a far-off roar can be heard, and now the way tops a forested crest—and below are the loud breakers and beyond is the vast Pacific horizon. The trail quickly drops to the beach of Cape Alava, 3½ miles.

Camping space for scores of people (but often overcrowded in summer by hundreds of people) is available on a grassy wave-cut bench, the site of an Indian village occupied for centuries. There are many, many ghosts here; archaeologists have excavated houses buried in a mudslide 500 years ago; other buried houses, dating back at least 2500 years, are awaiting excavation. Artifacts are on display in the Makah Museum in Neah Bay. For sidetrips, explore at low tide out onto Ozette Island and Cannonball Beach, covered with large, round concretions, or hike 1½ miles north to the Ozette River and a far look toward Point of the Arches (Hike 97).

The beach south 3 miles to Sand Point is easy walking at anything less than high tide and offers an assortment of sands and rocks and tidal pools; camps and dependable water at several places. Halfway is Wedding Rock, inscribed with Indian petroglyphs. A few yards of boot-beaten track allow high-tide passage around the rock.

In trees along the beach south of Sand Point are countless good (and in summer, crowded) camping areas. For sidetrips south, see Hike 99.

To complete the loop, find the trail in the woods at Sand Point and hike 3 miles to Ozette Lake, again on planks in lush brush and forest.

99 RIALTO BEACH TO CAPE ALAVA

One-way trip 22 miles	USGS Olympic National Park or
Allow 3 days	La Push and Ozette Lake
High point 100 feet	Park Service backcountry use
Hikable all year	permit required

Olympic National Park first became famous for rain forests and glaciers set within a magnificently large area of mountain wilderness. Now, though, it is known far and wide for still another glory—the last long stretch of wilderness ocean beach remaining in the conterminous United States. North and south from the Quillayute River extend miles and miles of coastline that are now almost exactly as they were before Columbus—except that in 1492 (and until fairly recent times) Indians had permanent homes and temporary camps at many places along the coast now deserted.

Winter and early spring often offer the best hiking weather of the year, but storms can be hazardous. Facing a cold rain with miles of beach to hike is miserable and can lead to hypothermia.

The north section, from Rialto Beach to Cape Alava, makes a longer but easier walk than the south section described in Hike 100. There are no really difficult creek crossings, only one headland that cannot be rounded at low tide, and most of the way is simple sand and shingles, interrupted occasionally by short stretches of rough rock.

Be sure to obtain a tide chart beforehand and use it to plan each day's schedule. Much of the route can be traveled at high tide but at the cost of scrambling over driftwood and slippery rocks, plodding wearily through steep, loose cobbles and gravel, and climbing up and down points. Moreover, some headlands cannot be climbed over and the beach at low tide provides the only passage. Be prepared to hike early in the morning or late in the evening, with layovers during the day, if the tides so dictate.

Also beforehand, pick up the Park Service brochure, "A Strip of Wilderness," which will add immeasurably to your enjoyment by explaining what you see and by helping plan a safe and pleasant trip.

Drive US 101 to 2 miles north of Forks. Turn west on the La Push road 8 miles, then turn right on the Mora Campground–Rialto Beach road 5 miles to the parking lot at the beach.

In ½ mile is Ellen Creek, the first possible campsite. Here and elsewhere the "ocean tea," the creek's water colored by bark tannin dissolved in headwaters swamps, is perfectly drinkable when treated as you would any other water found in the wilds. At 1½ miles, just beyond the sea stack with the Hole in the Wall, are meager camps and the first headland, which has several small points, one requiring low tide to get around. At 2½ miles are camps near the Chilean Memorial, which commemorates one of the countless ships wrecked on this rugged coast, and at 3 miles begins the long, rough rounding of Cape Johnson, which has no trail over the top and can be passed at low tide only, as is true of another rough point immediately following. A point at 5 miles must be climbed over on a short trail and one at 6 miles rounded at low tide. At 6½ miles is Cedar Creek (campsites) and immediately beyond is a point that can be rounded at low tide or crossed on a steep, short path.

At the Norwegian Memorial (another shipwreck and more camps), 7½ miles, a rough, abandoned trail leads inland 2¼ miles to Allens Bay on Ozette Lake. (There is no trail along the lake, so unless a boat pickup by the resort has been arranged, this is not a shortcut to civilization.) Passing campsites every so often and at 10 miles a low-tide-only point, at 13½ miles the way comes to Yellow Banks, the point at the north end of which must be rounded at low tide.

At 15 miles a way trail heads inland 2 miles to Ericsons Bay on Ozette Lake. At Sand Point, 15½ miles, are innumerable campsites in the woods and a trail leading 3 miles to the Ozette Lake road.

Don't stop here. Continue on the wilderness beach 3 miles to Cape Alava, 18½ miles, where an archaeological dig uncovered a Makah village that was overwhelmed by a mudslide 500 years ago. To finish your trip, follow the trail 3½ miles back to the lake, 22 miles.

Beach near Hole in the Wall

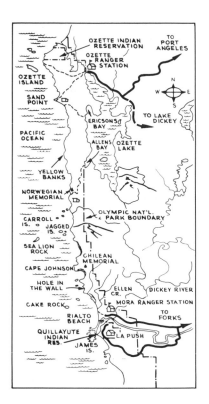

100 THIRD BEACH TO HOH RIVER

One-way trip 16½ miles
Allow 3 days
High point 250 feet
Hikable all year

USGS Olympic National Park or
La Push and Forks
Park Service backcountry use
permit required

Wild forest and wild ocean, woods animals and sea birds, tidal pools and wave-carved stacks, the constant thunder of surf, and always the vast, mysterious horizon of the Pacific. This south section of the Olympic National Park wilderness ocean strip is shorter but more complicated than the northern one described in Hike 99, requiring detours inland to cross headlands and creeks and demanding even closer attention to the tide chart.

Warning: Goodman, Falls, and Mosquito Creeks are high all winter, and after a period of heavy rain or melting snow are virtually unfordable.

Drive US 101 to 2 miles north of Forks. Turn west on the La Push road 12 miles to the parking lot at the Third Beach trail, elevation 240 feet.

Warning: Cars at the Third Beach parking area frequently have been broken into. Do not leave any belongings visible inside the car.

Hike the forest trail, descending abruptly to the beach and campsites at 1½ miles. Head south along the sand and in 1 mile look for a prominent marker on a tree above the beach, the start of the trail over Taylor Point—which cannot be rounded at the base. The trail climbs into lovely woods, dropping to the beach at 4 miles and a small head which can be rounded at any time except high tide; a path climbs over.

At 4½ miles is a point that can be rounded at low tide or climbed over by a short trail to reach Scott Creek, with campsites in the woods; another very small point immediately south can be rounded in medium tide or climbed over. At 5 miles is Strawberry Point, low and forested and simple, and at 6½ miles, Toleak Point, ditto. Shortly beyond is Jackson Creek (camps).

At 7½ miles a trail ascends a steep bluff and proceeds inland through beautiful forest to crossings of Falls and Goodman Creeks (cliffs rule out a shore passage), returning to the surf at 8¾ miles. The beach is then easy to Mosquito Creek, 10 miles; ford the stream at low tide. Camps here. There now is a choice of routes. On a *minus tide in calm weather* follow the beach, crossing four or five small points; less exciting but more

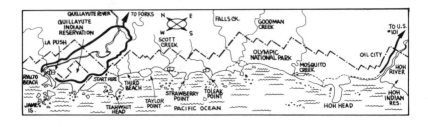

Toleak Point

certain, take the overland trail—keep careful watch on small children in the party, lest they sink without a trace in a mudhole.

At 13 miles a trail climbs the large promontory of Hoh Head, which cannot be rounded in any tide, and regains the beach at 13¾ miles. Going by a campsite or two, at 14½ miles the way comes to the last point, a heap of big rocks which must be rounded at low tide. From here a narrow, low-tide-only strip of beach leads to the mouth of the Hoh River, 15¾ miles. A trail follows the river inland to the Oil City road-end, 16½ miles. The Oil City road reaches US 101 in 12 miles, at a point about ½ mile north of the Hoh River bridge.

STILL MORE HIKES IN THE SOUTH CASCADES AND OLYMPICS

The 100 hikes chosen for description represent all provinces of the Cascades from Snoqualmie Pass to the Columbia River, and of the Olympics. They sample all areas presently protected as national parks, national monuments, and national wildernesses—and some that must be in future. However (praise be), there are countless other great hikes.

Below is an additional list—not comprehensive, merely suggested—of more hikes than are described in this book. To take them, consult the books referred to, if any, or obtain the applicable maps and make your own way. Some connoisseurs refuse to read our "recipes," preferring to go out on their trips uninformed and be surprised. The true purists don't even carry maps, not even of highways. Their sport is indescribable. Compromisers who choose their destinations from the list below rather than the descriptions above may be richly compensated by true wilderness, possibly even complete solitude.

CLE ELUM AREA

North Ridge trail No. 1321: From Cle Elum River valley to Windy Pass.

Big Creek trail No. 1341: Same trailhead as North Ridge, ends on Blazed Ridge.

Blazed Ridge trail No. 1333: Part of the Manastash Ridge trail system.

Manatash Ridge trail No. 1388: Follows the ridge between the Naches and Cle Elum Rivers over 20 miles.

WHITE RIVER

Huckleberry Mountain: A once-popular trail now nearly obliterated by logging.

Dalles Ridge trail No. 1173: Starts from trail No. 1184, 3½ miles of scenic trail with views of Mt. Rainier. Ties to road No. 72.

Ranger Creek trail No. 1197: Constructed by volunteers of the Boy Scouts of America. 8 miles to Dalles Ridge trail No. 1173. Good views overlooking White River in 2¼ miles. (See *Footsore 1.*)

White River trail No. 1199: 5-mile lowland trail in big timber paralleling Highway 410. (See *Footsore 1.*)

Deep Creek trail No. 1196: A steep 5 miles to Noble Knob trail No. 1184, the last ½ mile in open alpine country.

Lost Lake trail No. 1185: Starts 3¼ miles up the Greenwater trail, passes Quinn Lake, Lost Lake, and goes through alpine country to join the Noble Knob trail. Trail is 5½ miles long.

Maggie Creek trail No. 1186: Starts 5½ miles up the Greenwater trail. In 5¼ miles, all in timber, reach Pacific Crest Trail.

Arch Rock trail No. 1187: Steep 3½-mile access to Pacific Crest Trail starting 7½ miles up the Greenwater trail. Last ½ mile in alpine country.

Cedar Lake: Steep, 1-mile fishermen's trail to Cedar Lake in Clearwater Wilderness, then ½ mile more to Celery Meadow.

Rainier View trail No. 1155: From road No. 7174 at Corral Pass, 1½ miles to gorgeous views of Mt. Rainier and forest.

Bullion Basin trail No. 1156: From the end of Crystal Mountain road 2 miles to alpine scenery.

Divide trail No. 1172: From road No. (7038)330, a subalpine ridge walk crossing some clearcuts.

Suntop trail No. 1183: From Buck Creek road No. (7160)210, 8 miles crossing roads, clearcuts, and pleasant forest to Suntop Mountain. (Also reached by road.)

Silver Creek trail No. 1192: 1½ miles from Crystal Mountain road to Pacific Crest Trail.

Skookum Flats trail No. 1194: A 7½-mile forest walk paralleling the White River from Huckleberry Creek road No. 74. (See *Footsore 1*.)

Deep Creek trail No. 1196: 4 miles from Highway 410 to Noble Knob trail.

Palisade trail No. 1198: 6.6 miles from Highway 410 to viewpoints of falls and cliffs.

AMERICAN RIVER

Bismark Peak trail No. 983: Reached from Bumping Lake or Indian Creek trails.

Richmond Mine trail No. 973: Long route from Bumping River to Rattlesnake Creek.

Mt. Aix trail No. 982: A long hike from road No. 1502 near Meeks Table up the north side of Mt. Aix.

Pleasant Valley trail No. 999: A 13-mile loop trail starts and ends at Hells Crossing. It follows both sides of American River. It is also a cross-country ski trail in winter.

Cougar Valley trail No. 951: Road No. 182 intersects the trail. One way reaches the Pacific Crest Trail and the other Crow Lake.

TIETON RIVER

Little Buck trail No. 1147: Constructed in 1975, joining Indian Creek trailhead with Sand Ridge trailhead and allowing more loop hikes on the Tumac Plateau.

Sand Ridge trail No. 1104: Long, dry, flat, and wooded ridge hike from near Rimrock Reservoir to Blankenship Meadows.

Short and Dirty Ridge trail No. 1121: Not short but certainly dirty.

Tenday Creek trail No. 1134: Starts from Conrad Meadows. A long creek-and-ridge route to Cirque Lake. Just above lake is a fine view of Goat Rocks.

North Fork Tieton trail No. 1118: Forest trail to Crest Trail at Tieton Pass, not far from McCall Basin to the south, Shoe Lake to the north.

Divide Ridge trail No. 1127: From Jumpoff Lookout west to Darland Mountain. Hike early in season; little water after late July.

Round Mountain trail No. 1144: A ridge-top trail from White Pass to Round Mountain. (For the short way to Round Mountain see *Trips and Trails 2*.)

WILLIAM O. DOUGLAS WILDERNESS

Carlton Ridge trail No. 42: An alternative way to reach the Pacific Crest Trail from road No. 4510. Old-growth Douglas fir and some views.

Cramer Mountain trail No. 57: From road No. 57 to Pacific Crest Trail.

Cartright Point trail No. 60: From US 12 crossing of road No. 1284 to Sand Lake.

GOAT ROCKS WILDERNESS

Bluff Lake trail No. 65: Long route to Coyote Ridge and Goat Rocks Wilderness.

Trail No. 83: On Snyder Mountain, joining trail No. 86 in 1 mile.

Angry Mountain trail No. 90: Ridge hike to Lily Basin.

Glacier Lake trail No. 89: Steep trail from road No. 2110 to lake in Goat Rocks Wilderness.

RANDLE AREA

High Ridge trail: From road No. 29 past beaver ponds to Tongue Mountain trail.

Burley Mountain trail No. 256: Early-season hike from road No. 76 to snowline.

Wobbly Lake trail No. 273: From road No. 2208 past Wobbly Lake to road No. (7807)060.

Mouse Ridge trail No. 119: From road No. 78 to Blue Lake trail No. 271.

Strawberry Mountain (Ridge) trail No. 220: 6-mile trail up a forested ridge from road No. 26045 to road No. 2516.

MT. ST. HELENS NATIONAL VOLCANIC MONUMENT

Strawberry Mountain trail: From road No. 99 at Bear Meadow to a dramatic view of Mt. St. Helens' crater.

Vanson Peak trail No. 217: Best reached from Ryan Lake over Goat Mountain. North end of trail is in private land (U.S. Plywood–Champion Papers).

Vanson Lake trail: A 1-mile sidetrip from trail No. 217.

Green River trail No. 213: 9-mile trail from Ryan Lake to edge of monument. Scheduled to be reopened in 1986. Partly through blast area and partly through virgin forest.

LEWIS RIVER

Quartz Ridge trail No. 2: From road No. 90 to Summit Prairie.

Snagtooth Creek trail No. 4: Climb from Quartz Creek trail to Boundary Trail.

Wright Meadow trail No. 80: Through forest between roads Nos. 2327 and 93.

Trail No. 17: 2½ miles from road No. 9341 to Craggy Peak trail No. 3.

PACKWOOD AREA

Backbone Ridge trail No. 164: From road No. 1270 past tiny Backbone Lake to the Stevens Canyon road at the edge of Mt. Rainier National Park.

Teeley Creek trail No. 251: Can start on road No. 84 for longer hike to Granite Lake.

Pompey Peak trail No. 128: Sidetrip to view from Klickitat trail No. 7 (see Hike 35).

Dry Creek trail No. 125: From road No. 20 go 5 miles to 5456-foot Goat Dike for excellent views of the Cowlitz Valley.

South Point trail No. 123: A lookout site and a long ridge hike on a dry access route to Klickitat trail (Hike 35).

MOUNT ADAMS WILDERNESS

Cascade Creek trail No. 75: From road No. 23060 a 2-mile valley walk under the cliffs of Stagman Ridge.

Snipes Mountain trail No. 11: From road No. 8020, trail climbs along a lava flow 5 miles to alpine meadows and a junction with Round-the-Mountain trail No. 9

Cold Springs trail No. 72: 15-mile loop hike is possible by starting on trail No. 11, going to the Round-the-Mountain trail, following it westward to timberline, then down the timberline road to trail No. 72, to trail No. 40, and walking ¾ mile on road No. 8020 back to the car.

Divide Camp trail No. 112: From road No. 2329 to Pacific Crest Trail.

INDIAN HEAVEN WILDERNESS

Placid Lake trail No. 29: From road No. 65 a short ½ mile to Placid Lake, then another mile to the Pacific Crest Trail.

Thomas Lake trail No. 111: From road No. 65 to Pacific Crest Trail past numerous lakes.

East Crater trail No. 48: From road No. 6035 to Junction Lake, one of the most popular in Indian Heaven Wilderness.

Little Huckleberry Mountain trail No. 49: From road No. 66 to 4781-foot former lookout site.

TRAPPER WILDERNESS

Soda Peaks Lake trail No. 133: The lake is a stiff climb from Government Springs or a short hike from road No. 54.

WIND RIVER AREA

Paradise Hills trail No. 124: A very steep and difficult trail from road No. 64201 to a great viewpoint.

Grassy Knoll trail No. 147: From road No. 68511 to 3549-foot Grassy Knoll, part of the old Cascade Crest Trail.

Little Baldy Mountain trail No. 172: From road No. 41502, a partly jeep road to Silver Star Mountain.

Silver Star trail: Jeep road No. 4109 to a viewpoint of mountains, Vancouver, and wildflowers.

Star trail No. 175: From road No. 4107 to Silver Star Mountain, noted for its wildflowers.

Sleeping Beauty trail: From road No. (8810)040, a 2-mile hike to a 4907-foot promontory, a former lookout site with spectacular views.

SOUTH SIDE OLYMPIC PENINSULA*

Lower South Fork Skokomish River trail No. 873: From road No. (2325)019, a riverside walk of 14 miles, sometimes in clearcuts and sometimes in forest.

Church Creek trail No. 671: From road No. 2326, climb over a 3100-foot divide and drop down to road No. 2222 in 3½ miles.

Wynooche Lakeshore trail: From Wynooche Dam a 12-mile loop of Wynooche Reservoir. May have to ford the river.

Wynooche trail from road No. (2312)024: A quick access into the south side of Olympic National Park. The Wynooche trail is steep and rough through impressive forest and past numerous waterfalls and over Wynooche Pass. At 3¾ miles reach Graves Creek trail only 1½ miles from Sundown Lake.

EAST SIDE OLYMPIC PENINSULA*

Mt. Washington trail No. 800: Starts from Big Creek road No. 2419. An easy grade 1½ miles to ridge top. Does not go to summit of mountain.

Mt. Rose trail No. 814: Steep, strenuous climb 3 miles to within ¼ mile of the 4301-foot summit. For experienced hikers only.

Dry Creek trail No. 872: Starts from road No. 2351 near the park boundary. The first 1½ miles are along the shore of Lake Cushman. Ideal for family hiking.

Wagon Wheel Lake way trail: Located near Staircase. Trail is a steep (12 to 15 percent) 3-mile climb to a small tarn. Good views of Mt. Lincoln and upper Slate Creek Basin.

Putvin trail No. 813: Starts at head of Hamma Hamma valley near Boulder Creek. A long-abandoned trapper's trail to alpine country. Extremely steep (some rock scrambling) but offers access to Mt. Stone, Mt. Skokomish, and acres of flowers and wildlife.

Greywolf trail: 20-mile hike to 6150-foot Greywolf Pass and descent to Dosewallips. Can be shortened by starting at Deer Park.

---

*See *Olympic Mountains Trail Guide,* by Robert L. Wood.

Cameron Creek trail: Reached from the Greywolf trail. A very long hike to 6400-foot Cameron Pass and on over Lost Pass to Dose Meadows.

Six Ridge from near Big Log Camp on the North Fork Skokomish River trail: Long, steep, dry way trail to subalpine meadows. Elk country.

Dungeness River trail No. 833: Beautiful valley walk to Marmot Pass and Constance Pass.

Lower Greywolf trail No. 834: 7 up-and-down miles from road No. 2927 through magnificent forest and clearcuts.

Tunnel Creek trail No. 841: From road No. 2743, a steep 2¾-mile hike to campsites.

Mt. Zion trail No. 836: From road No. 2849, a 2-mile climb to a former lookout site and striking views.

NORTH SIDE OLYMPIC PENINSULA*

Grand Ridge trail: 8-mile ridge walk from Deer Park to Obstruction Point. Splendid alpine hike. Carry water.

Little River trail: Lovely and little-traveled 8-mile route to Hurricane Ridge.

Lake Creek: Begins at Heart of the Hills Campground, Loop E. 2-mile woods walk, no lake.

Cox Valley way trail: Starts 1 mile along Obstruction Point road. Trailhead not marked. Goes into Cox Valley.

P.J. Lake: A way trail starting at base of Eagle Mountain on the Obstruction Point road. ½ mile down to lake. Way trail not marked.

Storm King way trail: 1½-miles steep trail to viewpoint of Lake Crescent on side of Mt. Storm King.

Barnes Creek trail: Indistinct way trail through forest to Aurora Ridge trail. Fades out as it reaches 5000-foot Lookout Dome.

Aurora Creek way trail: 3½-mile shortcut to Aurora Ridge trail. Very steep.

Aurora Ridge trail: 16-mile ridge walk, mostly in trees, then down to Olympic Hot Springs. Some good views of Mt. Olympus.

Long Ridge trail: From the Elwha trail to Dodger Point, a long, dry ridge with views. Ends in scenic meadows. Route to Bailey Range. Good trail.

Boulder Lake trail: 3½ miles from Olympic Hot Springs to Lake Crescent.

Happy Lake Ridge trail: Long hike with views and a lake, starting from Olympic Hot Springs road. Can be a loop with the Boulder Lake trail. 3½ miles between trailheads.

Martins Park way trail: 2-mile sidetrip from the Elwha trail at Low Divide to glorious meadows and views.

WEST SIDE OLYMPIC PENINSULA*

Geodetic Hill trail: Very indistinct route, abandoned in 1945, from the Bogachiel to forested Spruce Mountain.

Hoh-Bogachiel trail: Follows the park boundary from the Hoh over and down into the Bogachiel at Flapjack Shelter.

Indian Pass trail: Forested route from the Bogachiel River to Calawah River and on to Rugged Ridge and Forest Service road.

South Fork Hoh trail: Short trail to canyon. Very easy. Fades out in unspoiled rain forest. Trailhead difficult to find.

Mt. Tom Creek trail: A difficult ford of the Hoh River leads to seldom-visited forest.

Queets River trail: A difficult ford of the Queets River leads to 15-plus miles of primitive rain forest.

Kloochman Rock trail: From Queets trail past largest Douglas fir tree to lookout site. Officially abandoned.

Tshletshy Creek trail: From the Queets to Quinault; not maintained and very difficult to follow.

Elip Creek trail: Intersects the Skyline Trail from North Fork Quinault. 4½ miles.

Skyline Trail: Long, strenuous, scenic way trail to Low Divide. A late-summer trip, since snow obscures route at head of Promise Creek. Minimal way trail between Seattle Creek and Kimta Creek.

Three Lakes trail: Starts at North Fork Quinault Ranger Station. A 7-mile trail connects at divide above Three Lakes with Tshletshy Creek trail 18 miles from Three Lakes to Queets River.

Graves Creek trail: 9-mile hike from the Quinault to Six Ridge Pass and Sundown Lake.

Rugged Ridge trail No. 882: A steep climb from the Sitkum River over a 2000-foot pass on Rugged Ridge and then a steep descent to the Calawah River in a remote and seldom-visited section of Olympic National Park.

INDEX